Trotsky in Mexico
1937-1940

Alain Dugrand has published two novels, *Le désemparé* and *Une certaine sympathie* (Roger Nimier Prize). Associated with the founding of the daily paper *Libération*, he was a journalist until 1981. He 'discovered' the life of Lev and Natalia Trotsky during his many trips to Coyoacán. With Patrick Le Gall, Alain Dugrand has made two films about Trotsky.

James T. Farrell (1904-79), a naturalist novelist best known for his trilogy concerning Studs Lonigan, was one of the first to join the American Committee for the Defence of Leon Trotsky, and travelled to Mexico a number of times, forming a friendship with the exile in Coyoacán. He remains one of the major figures of the liberal Left in America.

Pierre Broué is professor at the Institute for Political Studies in Grenoble. Director of the Institut Léon Trotsky, he has published some twenty works, among them *Histoire du P.C. de l'URSS, Ecrits à Prague sous la censure, La Révolution espagnole*. He is editor of the French edition of Trotsky's works, and his monumental biography of Trotsky was published by Fayard in 1990.

.

TROTSKY
IN MEXICO

text by Alain Dugrand
portrait by James T. Farrell
afterword & chronology by Pierre Broué

translated from the French by Stephen Romer

CARCANET

First published in Great Britain in 1992 by
Carcanet Press Limited
208-212 Corn Exchange Buildings
Manchester M4 3BQ

A CIP catalogue record for this book is
available from the British Library
ISBN 0 85635 881 9

The publisher acknowledges financial assistance
from the Arts Council of Great Britain

Set in 11pt Palatino by Bryan Williamson, Darwen
Printed and bound in England by SRP Ltd, Exeter

to Felix Ibarra and Octavio Fernández, the faithful

Trotsky arrives at Tampico

Contents

Behind Natalia and Trotsky, those who came on board to greet them: Frida Kahlo, Max Schachtman, and General Beltrán, representing President Cárdenas.

Calle Viena, Coyoacán
Alain Dugrand

1981; Mexico; the old quarter in the centre of the capital. I had found a room in the Ontario Hotel, and for three weeks I walked the long streets of the city, mapped out by the conquistadors, to get to the Lerdo de Tejada Newspaper Archive to work on the collections there. On the way, pleased and impatient to get down to work, I pushed my way down the pavement of the street dedicated to Isabella the Catholic, avoiding the shoe shiners and the steaming hot pans of frying *tamales* – maize fritters stuffed with banana or meat. At ground level, on the burning braziers, blue tortilla were heating up, scenting the air with their strong aroma. Piled high along the fronts of the buildings, crates of Coca-Cola, Cidral and orange soda waited the arrival of the street-seller who would put them in his zinc ice-box and wander among the generous, childlike, busy crowd in the midst of the greatest metropolis in the world.

On my first visit, it took me a few minutes to realize that my library was where it was... Behind an incredible, baroque façade embellished with cornices, pediments, medallions, spirals; wreathed foliate columns; statuettes in profusion – Saint John the Baptist or Madonnas in adoration. A cathedral? The front of a Thai palace, a Spanish caprice... I took my place joyfully beneath the glass-plated ceiling, in front of my bound sets of newspapers from the nineteenth century, ready to discover something of overwhelming Mexico.

Books are never as beautiful as they are in libraries, whether in great national collections or in those of enlightened amateurs, in universities or private institutions such as in Tucson or in Paris in the rue Las Cases. Who can describe the happiness to be experienced in the whispering ambience of these

9

modern temples? 'The' Lerdo de Tejada had been a cathedral, destroyed at the beginning of the century by a murderous earthquake; fifty years later, a Mexican minister of finance decided to rescue the pillars and build a library on the site of the ruin. On the flagstones where discalced Carmelites and ragged beggars had advanced on their knees, elderly men of letters and students in jeans dug about in the past of their country.

I had decided to decipher an account of one *quatorze juillet* celebrated by the French Charitable Association in 1860 in the Alameda gardens, when I raised my tired eyes to some empty scaffolding placed against a canvas some twenty-five metres high on which a charcoal sketch had been made. The painter was not at work. The white zinc panel which was smudged with lead and charcoal seemed to plunge the frescoes – covering some two thousand square metres of the building – into mourning. On the ceilings, on the walls, in the spaces left by bricked-up stained-glass windows, was spread the history of world revolutions, from Cromwell to Spartacus, from the Bastille to Petrograd; the history of climactic moments of thought and meaning, from Mozart to Galileo, from Shakespeare to Michelangelo, from Voltaire to Karl Marx. A pastel-coloured ocean which depicted these utopias in great unfinished fragments awaited its painter, who was absent on that particular day.

In libraries, tired readers start to wander. A moment comes when the student needs to smoke, walk, idle. Then his eyes will linger on the figure of a pretty librarian, or stare into space, or at details of the décor. The Lerdo de Tejada library is richly distracting in this way . . . Two days later, shivering in the coolness, I caught a glimpse of the painter – a strange man dressed in a Ukrainian shirt buttoned at the neck, wearing boots, and fencing away on his fragile metal scaffolding with his fine tips, brushes and rollers, setting specks of ochre dust and Veronese green playing in the rays of sunlight. The atmosphere was studious and I lowered my head to browse through a volume of *Trait d'Union*, a review founded by a French exile, the liberal journalist – and die-hard Republican – Eugène Masson, who fled after 1848. From the rue Gay-Lussac or a barricade in the Marais to Mexico Ciudad...

A heavy hand on my shoulder startled me from my ghostly adventurers and then I heard in my native tongue: 'Good God! *Des canards français!* How did they get here?' The man sat down in the chair next to mine and introduced himself. It was Vlady Kibaltchich, son of the writer and revolutionary Victor Serge. With his grey hair tied back beneath a Polish sailor's cap and his handsome face partly obscured by snowy sideburns *à la* Durakin, he became part of the family.

And that is how, by a combination of Mexican chance and natural curiosity, Trotsky and the October Revolution entered my life that day in Mexico.

If France is my native land, Mexico is my second country, close to my heart, the land of infinite spaces, my New World, a new world born out of the crises that have convulsed Latin America. As it has been for so many exiles and rejects. Mexico is in some ways the Paris of Central America; it is moved by the sight of the exile who sets down his suitcase or bundle on the floor of the airport lounge or on the quayside. Whether he be Nicaraguan, Cuban, Spanish, Argentinian, Guatemalan, Puerto Rican, Haitian or Chilean, Mexico is open to him. A stinking *cuarto* in a downtown block to sleep in, a hotel room to revive in, and a colourful reception centre where the refugee – unwanted by the world – can begin to reconstruct his life. Fidel Castro and Che both lived here before the victorious revolution that brought down Batista; the Nicaraguan Sandino found refuge here; Spanish Republicans came here in their tens of thousands and found new purpose to their lives; the Jews and European opponents of Fascism – from Victor Serge to Marceau Pivert, from Otto Rühle to Gustav Regler – found asylum here when the Europe of Stalin, Hitler, Vichy or Mussolini forced into flight those for whom utopia was blood-red.

Vlady, the painter, whose philosophical and political language remained French, was a Samaritan who opened Mexico up to me. He took me to Coyoacán and led me beneath the hanging foliage into the garden where Trotsky is buried, in the Calle Viena. He introduced me to Esteban Volkov, known as Seva, grandson of Lev Davidovitch, the day he married one of his daughters. Thanks to Vlady, I had the joy of meeting that crowd of elderly revolutionaries, loved ones and friends of Lev Davidovitch Bronstein and Natalia Ivanovna Sedova, now buried together under the Mexican sky.

At times my presence among them seemed anachronistic. I have to confess that Trotsky is not my hero. I find it hard to forget the People's Commissar of the Red Army, responsible for Bolshevik repression from the populist-libertarians of the Makhno movement to Kronstadt; and then his followers who endlessly parade their theoretical grasp of very dated theses seem to me slightly ridiculous. And yet my growing familiarity with the work of historians who have studied the Left in opposition has led to a passionate interest in Trotsky, and in the fate of those thousands of men armed only with political and moral concepts who fell victim to the butchers of the Kremlin. And despite it all he remains that intransigent figure, a thorn in the flesh to those democracies all trying – in their struggle for survival – to establish the friendliest possible ties with Stalin, the Thermidorean.

Imagine it: from Norway to Mexico.

Oslo, December 1936. Endless snow. The fjords iced over, frozen sludge on the paved streets of the capital. The palace gardens, under a metre of snow, extend to the rococo theatre and falter at Ibsen's statue before halting at the parliament buildings.

Trotsky and Natalia are there, escorted by the police. They are anxious as they step on to the frozen gangplank of the *Ruth*. Soon Oslo is behind them, obscured by mist and winds from the pole. Mists? The fogs, rather, of Northern Europe mixed with frost and salt crystal: Oslo, engulfed in a few minutes, and the long voyage ahead.

In the mid-Atlantic, imagine them soporific from the throbbing of the engines, sickened by the smell of naptha which hangs everywhere, even though the holds are empty. But not seasick – the ocean is calm. They are merely two elderly

Europeans on the bridge of a Norwegian tanker *en route* for Mexico, which they have no idea of. Terra incognita. But Jean van Heijenoort, Trotsky's secretary, had gathered some basic information from the Bibliothèque Sainte-Geneviève in Paris about the country of Villa, Zapata and Obregón.

Natalia Ivanovna Sedova and Lev Davidovitch Bronstein have taken refuge in the personal quarters of the Norwegian captain, Hagbart Wagge. On board the *Ruth*, a singular passenger, the Nazi policeman Jonas Lie, confiscated the old man's revolver...

Trotsky is apprehensive about his arrival in Mexico. As usual, Natalia takes on the worries of her companion as well as her own. Twenty-one days at sea, with no friends and no news of their beloved shaken Europe, and only the sketchiest knowledge of their destination. Jonas Lie forbade any radio communication with Trotsky. There were to be no messages to New York or Paris. For the last time the Trotskys are being held prisoner – this time of the Norwegian Socialist government – on board a tanker heading for Tampico, a port on the Atlantic coast of Mexico.

In Norway, despite their possessing valid visas, the Social-Democrats had placed them under what amounted to house arrest in Sundby, on the first floor of a sordid building occupied on the ground floor by fifteen policemen. The Trotskys were confined to the courtyard and their correspondence was censored. A special law had to be ratified to legalize this unconstitutional internment.

Stalin's word was law. A Nazi commando, helped by Quisling's Norwegian Fascists, had wrecked their previous residence in Vexhall. It was then that socialist Norway, threatened with economic sanctions by the USSR, had decided to get rid of Trotsky: the old man's skin in exchange for cargoes of herring and pork. Moscow hammered out the message: 'The presence of Leon Trotsky in Norway must hinder normal diplomatic relations.'

'Planet without a visa'; the expression is Trotsky's. It has been attributed to Victor Serge and then to André Breton. Whatever the truth, both of them went knocking on the doors of all the chancelleries: who would accept Lev Davidovitch Bronstein on their soil? During those years, along with a few thousand others, Serge and Breton saved the honour of the species. It was indeed heroic, in the hour of danger, 'when midnight had struck in the century' – as Victor Serge put it – to adhere faithfully to the revolutionary utopia, in the teeth of Stalin's International, German Nazism and European Fascism. The democracies were afflicted with vertigo. France under Laval had made a pact with Stalin, the United States under Roosevelt was engaged in clandestine negotiation with Russia and the stage was set for Munich...

But why was Cárdenas the only political leader in the world to welcome Lenin's comrade? Adolfo Gilly and the other Mexican historians reply: out of moral integrity. The expression is archaic, if not dead, in Europe today, and it was scandalous at the midnight hour of the century.

Adolfo Gilly, Argentinian by birth, is now Mexican. Professor of political science at the National University of Mexico, he lives at Coyoacán, a few blocks from the Calle Viena where the ashes of Natalia and Lev Davidovitch repose. Gilly is a Latin-American Militant Revolutionary – the expression is hard to swallow in the palaces of old democratic Europe, I know. Adolfo Gilly, who knows the great cities of Central America, the dust clouds that blow through those *ciudades perdidas*, and who has known the prison cells, is still a revolutionary and at the same time a historian of the Mexican revolution. Quite serene, speaking in French which he had picked up during his four years of exile in Paris, Gilly described Cárdenas as he envisaged him.

"He protested against Mussolini's invasion of Ethiopia, he protested against the invasion of Austria and Czechoslovakia by Hitler, he condemned – and now I think he was right to do so – the invasion of Finland by Stalin. Trotsky defended the latter as a defensive necessity, which seemed obvious to him, but then Cárdenas was a nationalist not a Marxist... Above all, Cárdenas supported the Spanish Republic by

14

sending arms to the Republican camp – not of such good quality as those supplied by the Soviet Union, but supplied without political conditions...'

In the cool of Mexico University's *cinémathèque*, behind the ruins of Montezuma's palace, in the old historical centre of the city, I watch President-General Cárdenas welcoming hundreds of orphans from the Spanish revolution. In the State of Michoacán, not far from Lake Patzcuaro in Morelia, his nationalist government built villages for the orphans of that unhappy revolution, crushed by the joint forces of European Fascists and Soviet Stalinists and abandoned by the paralysed democracies. *Los Ninos de Morelia*, adopted by a revolutionary general, friend of Villa, Zapato and Obregón...At the same time, in France, hundreds of thousands of ragged Republican exiles were placed in detention camps this side of the Pyrenees, and guarded by gendarmes.

In sight of Tampico, Trotsky warned Jonas Lie that he would not disembark unless friends came to meet him, because he feared an assassination attempt by the GPU.

A big launch took them ashore. Trotsky looked like an English tourist, belted into his knickerbockers. Natalia, pale and fragile, encountered tropical Mexico. A group climbed up on to the bridge to celebrate their arrival. One of the group was the strange-looking Frida Kahlo, upright, haughty, outrageously made-up in Indian style, smoking a panatella. Her husband Diego Rivera, the world-famous artist, was in hospital and so unable to come.

Diego Rivera, Diego-de-Montparnasse, as one of his biographers nicknamed him...In Paris he lived through ten years of upheaval, all the aesthetic revolutions at the beginning of the century. Co-founder and veteran of the Mexican Communist party, he caused a major scandal at the Rockefeller Centre when his fresco portraying Lenin was torn down on the orders of his fabulously-rich employer...Stormy Rivera, enormous, hippopotamus-bodied; friend of Matisse, Picasso, Indian brother of Gaugin and the Douanier Rousseau.

Also on the pier at Tampico was George Novack, secretary of an American Committee for the Defence of Leon Trotsky, with numerous intellectual contacts in New York and Chicago. In 1934 Novack had tried to soften up the American authorities and persuade the United States to give political asylum to Trotsky.

'We went to consult Ernest Morris', he explained, 'legal adviser to the American Civil Liberties Union and a personal friend of the Roosevelt family. One Sunday evening he was dining with them in the White House, and at the end of the meal he said to Roosevelt: "I've got a friend and I would like to obtain political asylum for him." Roosevelt asked: "So who is this friend, Morris?" "Leon Trotsky", he replied... Taken by surprise, Roosevelt stubbed out his cigarette and said: "So ... That's a big deal... Before doing anything I'll have to consult the State Department." The latter refused to allow Trotsky into the United States. Stalin would have taken such an initiative as a supreme affront at a time when diplomatic relations between the two countries were being re-established.'

Three years later, in 1937, George Novack intervened once more for Trotsky, and it was thanks to him that Mexico under Cárdenas reserved such a generous welcome for the revolutionary.

The little crowd gathered under the hot sun was smiling and timid in front of the exile who was trying to put faces to the names he knew. There were a few dozen American and Mexican revolutionary militants, a few artists and... a high-ranking officer in uniform. He was General Beltrán, representing the Mexican government, and he took the couple to the station where, steaming away, President-General Cárdenas's private train was waiting. Cárdenas was the inheritor of the Mexican Revolution and, as the Mexicans like to add, the 'first of the century'... The train bore the name *Hidalgo*, in honour of the priest who rang the bell announcing the Indian and peasant revolt against the centuries-old authority of Conquistador Spain.

The Bolshevik-Leninist Leon Trotsky, considered almost as Lenin's brother by the muzhiks of 1917, afterwards exiled and rejected by all the European nations, from Great Britain to France, from Norway to the great democracy of North America, was welcomed on that day by a Central-American President-General, of nationalist and populist persuasion.

When the Old Man found himself on the pier at Tampico, blinded by the tropical glare, I imagine him completely beside himself, a passenger from the end of the world entering upon a renaissance...

'He thanked all of us, his American friends, for having obtained a visa for him, and we climbed into the central carriage of the *Hidalgo*. He was happy, and all the way to Mexico we talked of world events...In fact, with the soldiers of the Presidential Guard, we launched into a series of ballads from the Zapatan Revolution, and then he asked us to sing him some American songs so we thundered out *Joe Hill*, and Frida sang us some Mexican folk-songs...'

Today George Novack is a lonely old man. I met him in his modest New York flat one freezing spring day. Let it be said in passing that of those who were friends of Trotsky when he arrived on the American continent, very few have attained – fifty years on – wealth or eminence. In the photos of the time Novack appears as a slim, handsome man with one of those typically American faces that would much later become familiar to my generation via television and the cinema. He was representative of that rare and touching American intelligentsia, working class and anti-Stalinist, that defied the baseball bats of the mafiosi extreme right, and the police, when it demonstrated for the release of Sacco and Vanzetti; the brave libertarian left-wing making a chain in front of the Chicago docks while cops and thugs fired randomly into the crowd. Later its children were victims of the McCarthy purge, and its grandchildren, on the American campuses, burned army conscription papers in protest against the bombing in Vietnam...

Tampico, Mexico. Golden, burning Mexico; colour, the kindness of friends, the affecting grandeur of the one land offering asylum, under the governance of Cárdenas. And later, the gentler climate of Coyoacán in that quarter of the federal district which at the time was only a village.

17

Trotsky wrote: 'Having escaped a sickening atmosphere and a state of exhausting uncertainty, we found everywhere nothing but kind concern and hospitality.'[1]

The world had rejected Trotsky, the planet offered no resting place to Lenin's comrade, Commissar of the People, founder and organizer of the Red Army, pitifully alone now with his wife Natalia who held his hand as he walked cautiously down the gangplank of an empty petrol-tanker; the same man who, twenty years earlier, had commanded an army of five million men...

9 January 1937: a new scenario hoves into view for the President of the 1905 Soviet Executive in Petrograd. For three and a half years, under a clear sky, Trotsky was to tread the asphalt of Tampico jetty, until that last scene, a metal bed in Mexico's Cruz Verde Hospital.

Later, when Trotsky's ashes had been laid to rest, Natalia described the house Frida and Diego had lent them: 'A low, blue house, a patio filled with plants, cool rooms, collections of pre-Columban art, countless paintings.'[2] It constituted for them, a convalescence, a pause, an opportunity for hearts and bodies to mend.

From the first evening, Octavio Fernández, a Mexican teacher and member of the International Leftist Opposition, was present in the Blue House, avenida Londres, Coyoacán. Today, Octavio is an old man with black hair, with a blond cigarette permanently in the corner of his mouth. He lives modestly in one of those flowery villas which have sprouted in their thousands to the south of Mexico valley, on the edges of industrial complexes. 'That first night', he recalls, 'we were faced with the problem of security. So we decided to mount a guard ourselves, even though there were only three of us, Felix Ibarra, Diego Rivera and myself. So that night, we stood guard over Leon Davidovitch. Diego went home to get a Thompson machine-gun. I got hold of pistols, and we started on the first watch while Natalia and Trotsky, dead with exhaustion after their long journey, slept in Frida's house.'

Was it the Mexican sun, his new peace of mind, a let-up in the fevers and inexplicable stomach troubles that had plagued

18

Trotsky all his life? Whatever the reason, the fact is that a devouring passion was to develop, under the eyes of his entourage. Lev Davidovitch fell madly in love with Frida, the beautiful Frida Kahlo, Rivera's wife.

The painter Frida Kahlo was twenty-nine when Trotsky met her, badly disabled and obliged to wear a clinical corset after a terrible accident in her childhood. She was perhaps more disturbing than 'seductive'. Even today, flicking through the photographs of her, one is struck by her bold, cross-bred features and her deep, commanding eyes. She is so essentially Mexican. What did they see in each other? Trotsky at fifty-eight was certainly a very handsome man. He was tall, elegant, and always perfectly turned-out. But for the young painter there was the added romance and glamour associated with such a giant of history. And Trotsky? He was obviously caught up partly in amazement by the birth in him of such a passion at a time of life when, in his day, before the war, men were already considered to be old . . . Jean van Heijenoort, Trotsky's faithful friend, collaborator and bodyguard, recalls in his memoirs: 'Apparently he got caught up in it; he began to write her letters. He would slip the letter into a book and give the book to Frida, often in the presence of others, Natalia or Diego included, and recommend that she read it.'[3] It was a touching and absurd effort at seduction. . . . Life is surprising, chance provoking, but a veritable passion – wildfire or sheer curiosity – carried these two away in a mad clandestine affair. In June 1937, the liaison was no more than a flirtation: Lev Davidovitch met Frida in her sister Cristina's flat on the Calle Aguayo. As in all comedies the love interest was played stage left. Natalia suffered, his close friends and supporters muttered about a possible scandal. In the special confinement of exile it is not simple to obey such passionate promptings. And besides that, as Vlady put it, 'puritanism was and remains part of the Revolutionary Marxist Movement'. The old couple decided to separate. Trotsky took refuge in the arid desert of the San Miguel Regla plantation in the north of Mexico. This 'trial' parenthesis soon brought about the necessary break. . . . Lev Davidovitch, brought back to political necessities and the struggle he intended to pursue, moved apart from Frida.

The ensuing correspondence between Trotsky in San Miguel Regla and Natalia in Coyoacán outlines, in *pas de deux* rhythm, the necessary reconciliation between a couple whose lives were governed by history.

12 July. Trotsky: 'I imagined you coming to see me with all the feeling of youth, and embracing so closely, joining our lips, souls and bodies. I can hardly write because of my tears, Natalolschka, but could there be anything nobler than these tears? But I shall take myself in hand.'

13 July. Natalia: 'I took some Phanodorm. Three hours later I woke up feeling pierced by the same thorn. I took some drops. I'm so close to you, I cannot separate myself from you. Your little letters are my only "diversion", support and strength. They make me so happy, even though they're so sad. I can't wait to get home to read them.'

19 July. Trotsky. 'I have re-read your letter. "In the end, everyone is so terribly alone", you write. My poor, dear old friend! My darling, my beloved. But you haven't always been alone, and you aren't now; we're living for one another again, aren't we? Take heart, Nataloschka! I must get down to work. I kiss your eyes your hands your feet. Your old L.'[4]

The Moscow Trials and the persecution of the old revolutionary had mobilized American opinion in the 1930s.

The American Committee for the Defence of Leon Trotsky collected hundreds of adherents including such prestigious names as James Burnham, John Dos Passos, Max Eastman, James T. Farrell, Dwight MacDonald, Norman Thomas and, later, Edmund Wilson.

There was also, among their number, a young American militant by the name of Albert Glotzer, who had joined Trotsky on the island of Prinkipo in the Marmara Sea in 1931, bringing a suitcase full of homemade biscuits for Lev Davidovitch and Natalia.

Now in retirement in New York, Glotzer lives in a book-lined flat at the top of a skyscraper. He broke with the Revolution in 1940, having become convinced that democracy was the social system most likely to favour the emergence of working-class influence and power. For this jovial, loquacious reformer with cropped hair, bureaucracy – that deadly disease for society – is created by dictatorships, of whatever brand they may be.

For a large part of his life Glotzer was a militant member of the American Social-Democratic party. In his opinion the American Left was shattered by the First Moscow Trial.

'The event was incomprehensible, even for those of us who had left the Communist Party; for the independent Socialists, Unionists and Anarchists, the news coming from Moscow was unacceptable... Stalin and his entourage declared that all the former leaders of the Revolution, to a man, were counter-Revolutionaries who poisoned the workers' food, derailed trains and plotted against the lives of leaders of the Stalinist faction. They claimed that the Bolshevik Old Guard had been linked from the outset to the British, Nazi or Japanese secret services... And the traitor Trotsky was at the centre of this international plot against the Revolution! Naturally we rejected everything Moscow said, and we tried to set up a commission of enquiry with the purpose of refuting these lies.'

The popular struggle for the life of the two Anarchists Sacco and Vanzetti, which went on for seven years, and the later Rosenberg affair were firebrands to the American humanitarian conscience. No democracy in the world has given birth to a civil conscience as exigent, patient and at times even heroic. American cinema, literature and journalism testify to this incomparable civic spirit. Ernest Hemingway insulted Senator Joe McCarthy and his ally Cardinal Spellman during the anti-Communist witch-hunt at the start of the 1950s; in the 1960s the intelligentsia and student body protested against the Vietnam war, and clashed with the statist establishment in a wave of popular feeling unequalled anywhere else in the world; and in the 1970s, Nixon was unmasked as a plotter and manipulator by the journalist Woodward, a Robin Hood turned investigator.

In such a spirit, these young Americans of the 1930s took it upon themselves to make a counter-attack, and to inform the liberals of the true nature of the Stalinist Terror with its iniquitous trials and verdicts aimed at the destruction of the Bolshevik party and the massacre of thousands of men. In New York George Novack, James P. Cannon – head of the Socialist Workers Party – and the philosopher Sidney Hook sought out John Dewey. Dewey, then sixty-eight years old, was revered as one of the greatest thinkers and pedagogues of his time. Originally professor at the University of Michigan and then at Chicago, he taught at Columbia in New York from 1905 to 1929 and had considerable influence on the American intelligentsia. A disciple of Hegel, Dewey was a pure product of the American Liberal movement – that is to say, an authentic democrat.

In 1937, against the wishes of his family and his close friends, Dewey agreed to head an International Commission of Enquiry into the Moscow Trials in which Trotsky had been denounced as an 'agent of Hitler and the Japanese Emperor'.

On 2 April 1937, Dewey and his advisers boarded the Sunshine Special Express bound for Mexico where a team of technical experts had preceded them. They arrived on 6 April, but Dewey thought it wiser not to meet Trotsky just yet. He considered than any personal contact before the hearings would lessen their credibility. But he did receive the Mexican press – fascinated by the event – and devoted three days to lengthy work sessions. As to how the trial should be run, he consulted Albert Goldman, the Chicago lawyer appearing for Trotsky; Goldman replied that his 'client' would conform to the decisions of the Commission.

The proceedings were finally opened on 10 April 1937, in Frida's Blue House, efficiently guarded by the Mexican police. Sandbags blocked the entrances and patrols moved around Coyoacán to forestall any Stalinist provocation.

The hearings lasted from 10 to 17 April. In all, there were thirteen sessions in front of a public of around fifty people, for the most part journalists and special guests such as Jacopo Abrams, delegate of the Israeli Cultural League, and Luis

Sanchéz Pontón, Mexican correspondent for the Society of Nations. Sitting with Trotsky at his table was his lawyer, Albert Goldman, together with Natalia and his secretaries Jan Fraenkel and Jean van Heijenoort, responsible for producing or quoting from documents.

At the start of the first session, Saturday 10 April, Dewey made a brief speech. Having reminded the public that the court, along with millions of workers throughout the world, believed that 'no man should be condemned without the chance to defend himself', he paid homage to the Mexican government and its 'interpretation of political democracy' which made the hearing possible. He concluded: 'I have devoted my whole life to the work of education. Its business is to enlighten minds in the interest of society. I have accepted the responsibilities entailed as president of this Commission for one reason: to act otherwise would be to be false to my life's work'.[5]

Amid the turmoil of world events, with the Stalinists in Spain preparing to crush the Catalan Revolutionary Movement and eliminate the Anarchist chiefs and leaders of the POUM, Trotsky in Mexico, in front of the democrats, was determined to prove he was innocent of the crimes imputed to him by Stalin.

In 1936 Trotsky had invited the Soviet government to draw up a demand for his extradition because it would entail providing proof to support the accusations brought against him by the prosecutor Vyshinsky. The Soviet Supreme Court could have held the trial of Trotsky and his son Leon Sedov and condemned them *in absentia*, but that would have meant conferring some legitimacy upon them, and giving them a chance to defend themselves before international opinion. It would also risk tearing the tissue of lies masking the counter-Revolution the government was establishing. The calumnies perpetrated in groundless accusations, disseminated and exaggerated by the Communist parties and their associates, baffled the world. The few defenders of truth and justice were cast as wretches and villains. Courage and contempt for wounding lies counted for nothing.

Leon Trotsky's situation was extraordinary, to say the least. Ousted from power at the end of 1923, and from 1927 to 1929 under strictest surveillance in the USSR, he was expelled to Turkey in 1929, forcibly put on board the cargo-boat *Ilyich*. From then on he was cast as the leader of a vast conspiracy which included the majority of Russian leaders (even those who had persecuted him), the larger part of the Leninist party and tens of thousands of Soviet intellectuals, technicians and workers who had all, since 1917, joined the struggle against the coalition of the allied nations and the White Armies in league against the Octobrists...Having been a militant revolutionary from the age of seventeen and lived through two revolutions he was now obliged, in the eyes of the world, to defend himself against the charge of betraying his convictions, of concocting monstrous crimes, of collaborating with the Japanese and with Rudolf Hess's Nazis against the USSR...

The first task for the Commission was to hear Trotsky's testimony. It would then proceed to a cross-examination. With this in view, the Americans had gathered a preliminary group together, alongside John Dewey, including the radical journalist Suzanne La Follette, Carlton Beals, a university lecturer, and Ben Stolberg, an expert on the history of the labour movement, also Otto Rühle, formerly a Social-Democrat in the Reichstag. The Commission had a number of advisers, most notably the lawyer John F. Finerty, who had defended Tom Mooney and Sacco and Vanzetti. Celebrated American intellectuals were also in attendance, including Herbert Solow, John McDonald, the painter Dorothy Eisner, and the novelist James T. Farrell.

The confrontation was sharp and animated. This, for example, is how Trotsky replied to Ben Stolberg:

'Humanity has not yet succeeded in rationalizing its history. This is a fact. As human beings, we have not yet learnt how to rationalize our minds and bodies. True, psychoanalysis attempts to train us to harmonize the physical and the mental, but it has met with little success so far. At the same time, the question is not whether we can attain absolute perfection in society. For myself, it's a matter of finding out whether we can

24

make great strides forward without seeking to rationalize the nature of our history on the pretext that with every big advance mankind takes a step or even a big stride back. I greatly regret it, but I am not responsible for it. After the Revolution – the global Revolution – mankind very likely will be exhausted. For certain men or peoples a new religion might appear and so on. But I am certain our revolution will be seen as a great step forward, just as the French Revolution was. Certainly, it ended with the Restoration of the Bourbons, but not before the world had moved forward, having learned the lessons of the French Revolution.'[6]

The exchanges with Dewey were sometimes lively. For the American philosopher, Stalinism was identical to Fascism. In contrast to Trotsky, he regarded Stalinist dogma not as a monstrous deformation of Bolshevism, but rather its natural evolution.

'I would like to know', he asked Trotsky, 'what permits one to think that the dictatorship of the proletariat, wherever it be, will not degenerate into the dictatorship of the secretariat?'

Trotsky: 'The formulation is an excellent one, but I must protest that even if the dictatorship of the secretariat predominates in Russia today, it is nevertheless a very real progress compared with the dictatorship of the Tsar. Moreover, the dictatorship of the secretariat is brought about by the backwardness and isolation of the country. More civilized and less isolated countries will therefore undergo a healthier, more democratic and shorter-lived dictatorship.'[7]

Albert Glotzer kept the minutes of the sessions. From time to time he would look up, exhausted, from his typewriter:

'For seven days Trotsky spoke, in self-defence and on the attack. It was quite extraordinary... He learned the little English he knew from Max Eastman who taught him in Moscow during the 'twenties. In Turkey, when I was working in Trotsky's secretariat, he tried to dissuade me from returning to America. "Albert", he would say, "stay two months more, only two months, until I can really speak English." And there in Mexico, some six years later, he testified for days on end with almost unimaginable intensity... His own biography, the history of the Russian movement, the events of the Revolution, the White counter-Revolution, the struggle against Stalin, the growth of the Leftist Opposition, his exile, his deportation, his life in Turkey, France and Norway...not to mention the innumerable ideas and writings which poured from him in his fight against Stalin. The old fighter who was now isolated and in exile – formerly at the head of an army – and now in the protection of beardless youths. He was now, nevertheless, at the head of a new army, however meagre, and the instigator of a new anti-Stalinist policy, aimed at liquidating Thermidor and the Bolsheviks...There was not the slightest bitterness in his tone or in his thought which remained invigorating throughout. The way in which he decoded and nullified the system of bureaucratic terror is quite simply unbelievable...'

A few months after the end of the hearings, in August 1937, they were published in New York in a fat volume of six hundred pages under the title *The Trotsky Affair*. The book confirmed the inanity of Stalin's arguments. The novelist Edmund Wilson, entirely won over, published an article in *The Nation*; and this was immediately followed up by a former Communist leader, Bertram D. Wolfe in *The New Republic*. Wolfe's position is all the more striking in that he had believed the confessions of the accused in the Trial of the Thirteen in 1936. From this point on, however, and despite his disagreements with Trotsky, Wolfe acknowledged that he had been hoodwinked.

On 12 December the Commission finally handed down its verdict, which was publicly announced at a meeting organized in New York by the Defence Committee. Its conclusions minutely detail the tissue of impossibilities and fables that had been trumped up by the Moscow prosecutions. The Stalinist Trials were thrown out as fraudulent.

After a quarrel with Rivera, Trotsky and Natalia left the Blue House, and moved to the Calle Viena.

Coyoacán. At the intersection of Morelos and Viena streets, the blind walls look somehow drunken. With its rust and ochre stains, the house resembled the hull of a dilapidated steamer that should have been struck off the list but which is still just afloat, cracking the cement pavement. It is scarcely credible that these walls should have borne witness to the final drama of Trotsky's destiny.

It was a house with colonnades and capitals perched on volcanic rocks quarried from the porous bedrock of the high Mexican plain. It was almost a ghost house when the Trotskys rented it, a ruined bourgeois *folie* in a quarter since deserted. Nearby was a dried-up river, since covered over by a layer of asphalt. This is the motorway to the very heart of the city. The dusty road with its line of wretched houses built of adobe – sun-dried brick – no longer exists; it has been replaced by a long, shady avenue which is almost chic... The Calle Viena is surrounded quadrilaterally by streets bearing the names of Europe – Berlin, Rome, Paris, London. The house looked like a castellated fortress-cum-patched-up cargo-boat: above the pilasters, low brick walls of grey clinker, and tons of cement slapped anyhow on to the terraces. This was an emergency... Arrow slits, loop-holes, machicolations, wooden ladders leading to turrets, look-out posts, night-watches... The home of the man on reprieve was protected by Brownings, Mausers, Thompsons. Unassailable.

But... 'Nothing can stop the GPU' warned Jacson Mornard, *alias* Ramón Mercader, cynically, for he was even then secretly in league with them.

In Moscow, the mass purges were reaching a climax, and in Eastern Europe Stalin's iron fist, clad by the Communist parties, crushed its opponents, who were Trotsky sympathizers.

David Rousset, who was a young militant in the Leftist Opposition in the Seine Federation of the SFIO (French Section of the Workers' International) before the war, then deported, and later still author of *L'Univers concentrationnaire*, recalls with emotion the years of peacetime Stalinism.

'We knew about the assassinations, the murders at that time. The anti-Stalinists were massacred... It's impssible now to convey the hatred that existed between the Trotskyites and

27

the powerful Stalinist hierarchy! Today the PCF [French Communist Party] is an altogether gentler beast, we might describe it as a small reformist party, but at that time it had an extraordinarily extensive fighting and policing capacity. It was surrounded by *flics*! They were dangerous too, being themselves flanked by the Soviet police who were even more lethal, real killers... When one talks of such things now it all seems quite strange, used as we are now to democratic civilities – but that was Stalinism. The working-class grass-roots of the PCF did much to legitimize this tendency, claiming as it did to incarnate the destiny of the proletariat... We're talking of workers who struggled in conditions that today's generations haven't experienced and who had a militant capacity that no longer exists. Certainly, the workers' schooling was theoretically rigid, but it was decidedly superior to today's appalling post-Stalinist theory, which is intellectually poverty-stricken. The Stalinist discourse of the 'thirties may have been disarming in its sophistry, but at least it contained some signs of thought'.

The same Party was associated with the purges.

Leon Sedov, Trotsky's elder son, died in a Parisian clinic in February 1938. The man the GPU dubbed 'the kid' [*fiston*], was twenty-nine years old.

Gerald Rosenthal, co-founder of the Surrealist movement, militant Trotskyite and Leon Sedov's collaborator at the organizational headquarters of the International Opposition remembers:

'Leon Sedov, whom I shall always remember as Lyova, was a very lively, vigorous and expansive young man. He gave up his electrical studies to help his father, running the Communist International secretariat in Paris, and disseminating opposition texts in Russia and to the four corners of the earth. He operated through a network of contacts in Soviet commercial delegations where we had sympathizers. He was the man primarily responsible for maintaining open help-lines and links with the Russians in opposition, known as isolators at the time, who were imprisoned in labour camps. He was responsible for the secret correspondence in which an entire article would be transcribed on to an area the size of a postage stamp. In the different ports of Europe we were in contact with dockers who were themselves in contact with Soviet sailors. With exceptional devotion and tenacity he edited the *Opposition Bulletin*. Materially speaking, he helped Trotsky more than anyone. Along with his father, he was denounced, during the first two grand trials, as a criminal agent in an international conspiracy against the Soviet Union. During the third trial, the prosecutor Vyshinsky didn't utter his name, because Leon Sedov was already dead...'

By February 1938, Sedov was exhausted by the pressure of work and other hardships. Unlucky in his private life, in love with a married woman who lived apart from him, scolded by his father who was rarely pleased with his collaboration, he was suddenly hospitalized for appendicitis. At the decision of Lola Estrine, a doctor and the sister-in-law of one of his collaborators, Sedov was taken to the Mirabeau Clinic, run by White Russians, in the rue Narciss-Diaz, in the 16th arrondissement of Paris. In reality, as it later turned out during the inquest, the owner of this establishment was very suspect: Doctor Boris Girmounski, formerly a doctor for the GPU, emigrated legally from the USSR and bought the clinic for a bargain price.

Étienne Zborowski accompanied Sedov to the clinic. Zborowski was an agent in the control of the GPU. In the summer of 1936 he contacted Leon Sedov at his personal address, given to Zborowski by a French militant. Étienne could speak and write Russian and Sedov, initially annoyed at the intrusion, finally made the best of it and took him on.

The operation, which was carried out by a French surgeon, Professor Thalheimer, went smoothly and Sedov seemed all set to recover normally. Four days later, however, and totally unpredictably, Leon Sedov was found naked and semi-comatose, wandering deliriously round the corridors of the clinic. He died shortly after without regaining consciousness.

Jean van Heijenoort, the devoted friend in Mexico, recalls:

'When we went into Trotsky's room, Rivera went up to him and told him the news. Trotsky's face hardened, and he asked "Does Natalia know?" "No" replied Rivera. "I'll tell her myself", replied Trotsky. We drove off rapidly. I was in front. Diego was next to me and Trotsky, stiff and silent, sat in the back. At Coyoacán, he immediately shut himself up with Natalia in their room. Exactly the same ritual exclusion had taken place at Prinkipo, when Lev Davidovitch's eldest daughter, Zina, died. We passed them cups of tea through the door, which was kept ajar. On the 18th, at one o'clock in the afternoon, Trotsky gave me some handwritten sheets in Russian which he asked me to translate, type out and distribute to the journalists. In them he demanded an inquest into the circumstances surrounding the death of his son.'[8]

Marguerite Bonnet, editor of André Breton's collected works in the Pléiade edition, lives in the 12th arrondissement of Paris. After Trotsky's death, Natalia Ivanovna went several times to stay with her. For months at a time she would wander about in Paris, visiting theatres and museums, trying to recover the happiness she had enjoyed in Paris with her husband... Natalia finally died of cancer in Créteil, at the home of a doctor friend.

According to Marguerite Bonnet the death – or murder – of Sedov affected the couple deeply. But a second drama gnawed at them...

'She confided to me that the imprisonment of her second son Sergei had been one of the hardest things of all to bear. Sedov, or Lyova, as she called him, had died mysteriously in this clinic "run" by the GPU. It was a dreadful blow for her and Trotsky but it was, in a manner of speaking, in the order of things, in that Lyova had fought alongside them. Sergei, however, was an innocent victim, arrested solely because he was Trotsky's son. This fact afflicted both of them intensely. She told me that after his disappearance, when all news of Sergei had dried up, Trotsky had had fleeting thoughts of suicide, and said to her: "Perhaps if I were to die, they would set him free?"'

The last letter from Sergei is dated 12 December 1934: 'My general situation is grave – unimaginably grave.' The boy had never really been interested in politics. As a schoolboy, he never wanted to join the Young Communists; his loves were literature, music and sport. He was also developing a passionate interest in engineering. His parents were finally informed that he had been arrested in the autumn of 1935 and locked up in a cell for eight months before being deported to Krasnoyarsk. And from then on, silence...

Sometimes, sons are faithful to their fathers. In May 1987, in the Political Science lecture hall in the autonomous National University of Mexico, three of them gathered, deeply moved, to commemorate the fiftieth anniversary of the arrival of Leon Trotsky at Tampico. Present were Chuauhtemoc Cárdenas, son of the President-General, resistant and editor of the Mexican journal *Corriente democrática*; then there was Vlady, the son of Victor Serge, who himself reposes in the tropics; finally, Esteban Volkov, little Seva – Trotsky's grandson – whose family had been fifty years in Mexico, and who experienced terrible suffering in his youth.

On 5 January 1933 his mother, Trotsky's eldest daughter, was thirty years old when she double locked her door and turned on the gas... As a sufferer from tuberculosis, she had been authorized by the Soviet government to undergo treatment in Germany. In a state of nervous exhaustion she watched the Brownshirts parade through the streets of Berlin, had news, every day, of the dozens of arrests and hundreds of capitulations at the Moscow inquisitorial trials, and before long sank into despair. Just as Hitler, swept to power in a landslide electoral victory, prepared to take up the Chancellorship, she was told that she had been stripped of her Soviet nationality. At this point the young woman decided to take her life. She had no news from her husband, Platon Volkov, imprisoned somewhere in the USSR. In 1935, Trotsky received a copy of a letter from the deportee, his son-in-law. The latter had been condemned to five years' hard labour. He had thought of suicide and wrote, alluding to the temptation: 'I have made a new start, having gone some way down the road

31

of the old Lafargues and nearly rejoined our Zinaichka. [...]
I hope you will write to me about Sevika [Seva, his son], it
would give me much joy: give me news of his health, his
studies, his mischiefs. I learn nothing of all this from his
photos, which is painful. I kiss you, my little boy, and all of
you . . .'[9]

Trotsky and Natalia, almost alone, survived . . . Broken-
hearted, they were haunted in the Coyoacán house by the
forms of children and of friends, struck down by the firing-
squad bullets, tortured in the dungeons of the Kremlin. Their
most intimate thoughts were haunted by grief and shadows.
Lyova and Sergei had been killed; what would become of the
grandchildren? Trotsky's daughters? Vanished. And his first
wife Alexandra, his companion, gone too. His two sons by
Natalia? Murdered.

On 17 May 1938 André Breton and his friend Jacqueline arrived
in Mexico. Almost from the first instant, a passionate enthu-
siasm for the country overtook the poet. For him, Mexico,
'with its mountains, its flora, and its dynamism – a result of
the mix of races – as well as its highest aspirations, was
destined to become the Surrealist place *par excellence.*'[10]

Breton's journey came at a time of his life when he was
extremely hard up. André Laugier managed to fix a lecture
circuit for him under the auspices of the French Foreign Minis-
try. But as so often at the ends of the earth, French bureaucrats,
who were little white embassy penpushers, reactionary in art
and morally contemptible, neglected the 'lion-maned' poet so
celebrated by the Mexican intelligentsia. There was no one at
the port to welcome the travellers, no accomodation had been
arranged and no money at all was advanced . . . It was Diego
Rivera, once again, who offered the couple the use of a house
he had in Mexico City.

Rumours of the Moscow Trials had caused French artists
and the more generous revolutionaries to break definitively
with Stalinism. According to his companions at that time, Breton, deeply shaken by so much horror, was living through a

physical and moral collapse that he surmounted only with difficulty. Mastering his disgust at the self-accusatory confessions of innocent men, he sided resolutely with the Socialists, Libertarians, Trotskyites and revolutionary Syndicalists who had determined to break with the French devotees of Stalinist counter-revolution. A handful of intellectuals and writers, most notably Jean Giono, Victor Margeuritte and Marcel Martinet, joined the militants on the Committee of Inquiry into the Moscow Trials, convened in Paris at the beginning of October 1936.

Since the fourth issue of *Révolution surréaliste*, dated October 1925, in which Breton published an enthusiastic article on Trotsky's *Lenin*, the bond of loyal admiration between poet and revolutionary had never been broken. The journey to Mexico, as blood flowed in Moscow, provided a chance for the two men to meet and, who knows, act together.

The context looked ominous, with the union of Fascist and Stalinist forces looming on the horizon, and with Trotsky isolated in Mexico. Now the latter saw in Breton a heaven-sent chance to help him to get through to the mass of Stalinist intellectuals and fellow-travellers who had been shaken by the successive waves of Moscow Trials. The PCF, at any rate, had clearly foreseen this, because the Paris branch organized a libellous campaign against Breton even as he was crossing the Atlantic *en route* for Mexico.

At Coyoacán, Trotsky – who was himself under fire, attacked and libelled by the local Stalinist chiefs Lombardo Toledano and Hernan-Laborde – came to Breton's aid by asking Jean van Heijenoort to organize a bodyguard during Breton's lectures, which were liable to sabotage by the devotees of Moscow. So it was that the Mexican construction workers, who belonged overwhelmingly to the Leftist Opposition, discreetly surveyed the arrangements during the first talk given by the poet at the Palace of Bellas-Artes. And the good Rivera, who was always an ardent and courageous defender of Breton, used his immense prestige to humiliate, in the Mexican press, those whom he dubbed 'the Stalinist intellectual clerisy and GPU-ists'.[11] Breton, he argued, was undergoing the same kind

33

of persecution that was victimizing Freud: thus the Fascist systems had joined and become as one. Moreover, he added, history would prove that between Adolf Hitler and Joseph Stalin there was absolutely nothing to choose. Rivera hailed Breton as a 'lover of Mexico, who has understood the mixture of beauty, grief, oppressed strength and black humour that seethes and burns in this country...'[12]

Trotsky and Breton, both disgusted by the enfeeblement and the submissiveness of art in the USSR, which was strictly proletarian from that time on, decided to set to work and produce what has come down to us as the *Manifesto for an Independent Revolutionary Art*.

Trotsky considered the novel to be one of the highest forms of art,. 'The novel is our daily bread', he had written in an essay on Gogol,[13] and he didn't hesitate to place the French novel on a level with the Russian. Breton's aversion to the genre is well known... Had he not, in the *Surrealist Manifesto*, anathematized novelistic fiction as guilty of corrupting the faculties of imagination and wonder for the wretched pleasure of describing trivial banalities? Trotsky had admired Louis-Ferdinand Céline's *Voyage au bout de la nuit*, whereas Breton had torn it apart. For the latter, every line of the *Voyage* demonstrated only the physical and mechanical facility of holding a pen and dipping it in filth...

The two men were also said to have had serious discussions about psychoanalysis. If Trotsky, along with many Bolsheviks, had hailed the contribution made by the Vienna school of Freud, Adler and Jung, he stressed above all the light they had thrown on 'the role played by the sexual element in the formation of individual character and social consciousness'. On the other hand, as far as art was concerned Trotsky remained stubbornly reserved. Psychoanalytic criticism seemed unworkable because for him – as indeed for Freud – it was indissociable from the practice of psychoanalysis.

Throughout his essay on Gogol, for example, he takes issue with those critics who see in the strangeness of his writing, in 'his melancholic disposition and his mystical ideas, a classic case of clinical psychotic depression. Why and how did this realist become a didactic mystic? It is not psycho-pathology but social history that will enable us to answer this question' he affirms.[14]

Breton later recalled his talks with Trotsky on the edge of Lake Patzcuaro, as they walked the length of a gallery that opened on to a miraculously coloured patio 'out of which rose the sound of mockingbirds from twenty cages'. He watched that restless, delicate hand 'which had commanded some of the momentous events of our times, stretch out to pat a dog wandering around us'. As he walked, Trotsky began to discourse on the loyalty of animals. Was he not a proven huntsman? Breton goes on:

'He could come to love an animal, and confer on it qualities of natural goodness. And like everyone else he spoke of devotion... At this point I tried to point out to him the arbitrariness attached to the attribution of feelings to animals that only really make sense in relation to man. And by the same token they accuse the mosquito of deliberate cruelty and the crayfish of deliberate backwardness. It was soon clear that he was unwilling to follow my reasoning. This weakness in his logic is moving in retrospect, since the loyalty of the dog was, in the widest sense, equivalent to the absolute loyalty of men to his own cause, for which so many had paid with their lives. This was "friendship" in the deepest sense.'[15]

Towards the end of May 1938, Trotsky suggested that he and Breton should plan a common manifesto under which revolutionary writers and artists could unite.

It was then that a strange thing happened, which Maurice Nadeau, at that time a militant Trotskyist and friend of Breton, has recounted strikingly: 'He [Breton] became aphasic for a few days, paralysed, unable to express himself or even write; he was completely deprived of his powers. He was blocked by having Trotsky breathing down his neck, as Jean van Heijenoort aptly put it. And the delay which Breton was guilty of, in Trotsky's eyes, led to a brief and violent quarrel between the two men.' The eagle and the lion, as a Mexican critic expressed it.

After this incident, there was a distinct cooling between the two men which lasted several days, but their friendship proved the stronger, and they were soon on good terms again.

Later on, during the return voyage to France, Breton wrote to Trotsky explaining this strange crisis:

'*Très cher Lev Davidovitch*, I have often wanted to address you this way but have lacked the confidence in your presence. If I mention this lack of confidence, it will help you better to measure the extent of the inhibition which paralysed me every time there was question of doing something in collaboration with you and under your scrutiny. This inhibition exists primarily, and you must at all costs understand this, because of my boundless admiration for you. It must have seemed, latterly, quite the reverse. I have often wondered what would happen if, by some impossible chance, I found myself face to face with one of the men on whom I have modelled my thought and sensibility. Rimbaud or Lautréamont, for example. I felt suddenly deprived of my powers, and prey to a sort of perverse need to hide. It's what I call, remembering King Lear, my Cordelia complex. Don't mock me for this, it is an absolutely instinctive reaction, which is, I have reason to believe, ineradicable. Now you yourself are one of those great men, perhaps – if Freud is dead – the only one living. But I shan't bore you any more with these personal explanations. Let them serve, merely, to explain our misunderstanding on the way to Guadalajara, which you are quite right to want to bring out into the open.'[16]

Finally, before he left, Breton managed to submit his text to Trotsky, written in green ink. It was discussed and altered during many working sessions. Sticking to his usual working method, Trotsky cut up Breton's manuscript and pasted extracts from it on to his own manuscript, typed in Russian. He then added his annotations in ink. Finally, the whole text was translated by Jean van Heijenoort.

The *Manifesto* is a perfect example of fusion between two strands of thought, two conceptions of intellectual creation. The original manuscript, now in the Houghton Library, concluded with the formula used by Trotsky in *Literature and Revolution*: 'Art must enjoy total licence'. Breton had wanted to add 'except against the proletarian revolution'... When he got back from Mexico, Breton explained that Trotsky had warned him of the use a bureaucratic dictatorship could make of that last phrase. The old Revolutionary had exclaimed: 'No! There must be no restriction of that kind. To admit it would be to mutilate art.' And Breton crossed out 'except against the proletarian revolution' without the slightest hesitation.

In his *Revolution Betrayed*, written two years before meeting Breton, Trotsky still held to this restrictive concept, but since that time, the kangaroo courts and bloody executions in the USSR had demonstrated just how far the bureaucracy was prepared to go in its hatred of revolution and liberties. In an issue of the American journal *Partisan Review*, dated June 1938, Trotsky wrote: 'The art of the Stalinist epoch will go down in history as the most spectacular expression of the profound debasement of the proletarian revolution. It is an art whose only function is to glorify the leader.'

Jean van Heijenoort has described the last meeting between the two men. 'Just as the two men were about to separate, on the sunny patio of the Blue House in Coyoacán, among cacti, orange-trees, bougainvillaea and pre-Columban idols, Trotsky went to his office to fetch the joint manuscript of the *Manifesto* which he gave to Breton. The latter was very touched. This was a very unusual gesture on Trotsky's part, unique even in the whole period I lived with him.'[17]

In the first days of 1939, as soon as he got back to Paris, Breton set up the *Fédération internationale de l'Art indépendant*, with Maurice Nadeau as secretary. Benjamin Péret, Jean Giono, Marcel Martinet, Henri Poulaille, Ignazio Silone and Jef Last joined it. Gide refused to lend his name, others wriggled out of it, like Roger Martin du Gard, and Breton was upset at the defection of Gaston Bachelard, who claimed he was not qualified to make a judgement in the matter...

May 1987. Sitting in front of the house near the dried-out pool, where old Leon had his domain... The huge trees are still loud with birdsong. It whistles, clucks and coos while the rising sap, in the garden at Coyoacán, encroaches on any free space.

Trotsky never saw this explosion of green – the banana-trees must have tripled in size. The façade of the house is barely visible, loaded with clouds of pink, carmine, gold and blood-red bougainvillaea. Creepers with royal blue flowerlets cover the dark, damp vegetal depths that provide hiding-places between walls, doors and windows. Windows? With steel shutters, and casements reinforced with bricks and blocks of stone, designed to guard the Bronstein family and their unpaid Mexican soldiers, devoted to the cause of Leon Davidovitch.

From time to time the old man liked to go for drives, flanked by his armed bodyguards and another car which contained, under cover, a Mexican officer. Trotsky, Natalia and the other friends would go for picnics in the Desierto de los Leones, in the Pedregal, in the strange fields of lava-flow to the north, on the way to Queretaro, or in the desert solitude of the Taxco plain. Sometimes they went as far as the edges of Hidalgo State, where Natalia liked to gather armfuls of orchids. Trotsky and his friends, with picks and buckets on their shoulders, would attack the cacti... Specimens of fifty, even eighty kilos would be loaded into the saloon cars, to be planted at Coyoacán. There was one species that especially fascinated Trotsky: the *viejitos* or 'little old men', an elongated cactus covered with white strands like snowy hair.

Every morning he would devote an hour to feeding his rabbits with an almost scientific meticulousness which must have exasperated his entourage and intrigued his Mexican friends. The rabbit is not a farm-animal in Mexico, and the idea of eating rabbit flesh provokes a general incredulous hilarity. These European customs...

He ground his own grain, carefully calculating the quantities required for the well-being of his rabbits. Up at six, he would clean out the hutches and enclosure and inspect the animals for any signs of illness or parasites. The activity provided a relaxation, certainly, but also an indispensable source of food for the numerous household of friends and collaborators who converged on Coyoacán.

There is a colour film of him, made by Alex Buchman, an American of the militant Left. Trotsky is there, holding himself as straight as a young man, gloved, changing the rabbit straw. He is wearing a well-cut fawn jacket and is alert in his movements. It's hard to believe that he's in his sixties. His hair is wild, his face tanned and his eyes a piercing blue. He is a tall man, in startling contrast to the Stalinist or anti-Semitic caricatures published in bourgeois papers, that present him as sickly and convulsed. Lev Davidovitch Bronstein was a handsome man. A 'dandy' as Vlady Kibaltchich calls him. His father, Victor Serge, told him Lenin's joke about the Head of the Red Army in the midst of Civil War: 'Do you know what LD would reply when asked by the officer in charge of the firing-squad if he had any last wishes? "Do you happen to have a comb, Sir?"'

During those last two years, his life was run with the regularity of a metronome. Farm chores in the morning, then his office until lunch. Except when under orders from his doctor (Diego Rivera's brother), no rest after lunch: group work fixed at one o'clock, followed by solitary study. In the evening, a second visit to the rabbits, then the office again – which he dubbed his 'prison' – before the communal dinner in the dining-room. It was a monotonous, exacting routine. When meetings took place in the 'prison', and a latecomer had to knock on the door, Trotsky would stop the conversation, get up, take the key out of his pocket and admit the culprit...

Trotsky was now sixty. 'He is alone', wrote Natalia who added this terrible sentence: 'We wander round the little tropical garden of Coyoacán surrounded by ghosts with gaping foreheads...'[18] Sometimes his wife would hear him, alone in his study, sighing deeply and speaking aloud to himself 'I'm tired, so tired...I can't go on!' Friends would come upon him in the garden, in solitary colloquy with famous shades, their skulls pierced by the executioner's bullets, former friends who now repented of that friendship, loading themselves with lies and infamies, maligning and accusing Lev Davidovitch, humiliating themselves in a kind of orgy of loss, without hope of any conceivable 'pardon', but offering their imaginary crimes up to their killers as a kind of testimony, perhaps, to their despair. There is Rakovsky, the dear friend and Soviet ambassador in Paris; from a princely family, he had given his entire fortune to the Russian revolutionary cause – and he came back deliberately to give himself up to Moscow and disappear in its dungeons, dressed in the one threadbare suit left him by the GPU. And there were Smirnov, Sosnovsky, and Muralov, the magnificently moustached general, hero of the Red Army, who had written, when he had plunged into the struggle of the opposition, that the waters of the Irtysh would have to flow from the sea back to their source before he would recant. And Kamenev, and all the rest... They had died in the most atrocious circumstance of all, having betrayed their better conscience and abandoned all dignity.

With an old-world discretion, and a frantic idealism, Trotsky never admitted to experiencing personal tragedy... He went on living, writing, publishing, alerting the workers and intellectuals of the world who seemed to have gone deaf, almost screaming out of sheer humiliation, with the sense, always, rooted in his soul, that he was the sole survivor of a decimated army. And yet, for him too, death was lying in wait.

Some years earlier, when he was in Domesne near Grenoble, writing his *Diary in Exile*, Trotsky tried to weigh up, as it were, the volume of Stalin's hatred for him. He wrote:

'Stalin would pay dearly, at this moment, to repeal the decree that banished me; how pleased he would be to mount a show-trial. But you cannot revoke the past; he will have to resort to using methods... other than a trial. And Stalin is obviously seeking these. But the danger of being unmasked is too great: the mistrust of workers in the West for Stalin's machinations can only have been intensified by the Kirov affair. Almost certainly with the co-operation of White organizations which have GPU agents working at the heart of them, or with the help of the French Fascists who are not hard to meet, Stalin will definitely resort to an act of terrorism in two cases: under threat of war, or if the opposition to him grows extremely intense. There is most probably a third or fourth scenario. *Qui vivra verra*. If it's not us, it will be others.'[19]

So much water had gone under the bridge since those lines were penned – 20 February 1935. Trotsky's prognostic was conservative... From 1936 onwards, far from recoiling from the unspeakable, Stalin had gone beyond it with his trials. The Spanish Civil War had widened his catchment area for recruiting killers, thereby easing the pressure on his own 'white' workforce, which formerly he had employed exclusively... As Pierre Broué has commented: 'At the start of the European War, the threat posed to the USSR by a Germany at loose in the West was sufficiently real to hurry [Stalin] towards the "act of terrorism" – on which, apparently, he was already resolved. Trotsky, in fact, was a condemned man after the German-Soviet pact, at the very latest.'[20]

On 19 May 1940, the *Voz de Mexico*, the main organ of the Mexican Communist Party, devoted an article to the 'old traitor', as Trotsky had been dubbed one day by the Party's General Secretary., Lombardo Toledano. The article was extremely violent and demanded Trotsky's expulsion from Mexico for his 'anti-proletarian and anti-Mexican activities'. General Cárdenas found himself under attack from two flanks – the pro-American Mexican bourgeoisie and the Stalinist Party. In the event of an attempted putsch, like that in the mountains led by General Cedillo, the Stalinist press would accuse Trotsky of inspiring it. The old man was astonished to read in the papers that the Euro-American petrol companies in Mexico had been nationalized: in the right-wing press, Cárdenas was consequently likened to a lifeless puppet, caught in the toils of the Red exile... Yet Trotsky never once met the President during his years in Mexico.

Despite everything, Cárdenas stood firm: the revolutionary was the guest of the Mexican people, whatever the opinion of lobbies controlled by foreign influence.

On 24 May 1940, at four in the morning, there was an armed commando raid on the house at Coyoacán. That night, four cars parked a block down the road from Trotsky's house, and their occupants soon converged upon it. They were dressed in police and army uniforms, and led by the painter David Alfaro Siqueiros. In a trice they overwhelmed and tied up the few guards from the Mexican police force posted there, night and day, in the likelihood of such an event as this. The raiders then proceeded to cut the telephone lines and the electric alarm system linking the house to the central police station in Coyoacán.

In the villa itself, however, every precaution had been taken to avoid the night guards being paralysed by enemy forces. The man posted behind the door was meant to pull one bolt only, which opened a grille, and then ask the visitor's name. If he was expected, the latter would then pass into a small vestibule also controlled by an electric button in which, once again, he had to show his colours. According to the members of the enquiry, the young American guard, Bob Sheldon Harte, keeping the watch that night, must have opened the door at the first ring of the bell. Was he in league with them? Was he a GPU agent, as some claimed later? We shall probably never know. For all that, Trotsky defended him to the very last. Natalia also retained her esteem for him, describing him as a boy of twenty-three, an idealist in love with Mexico.

Once through the door, the attackers made for the garden. One of them, armed with a Thompson machine-gun, dashed towards a big tree where he took up position, firing a round at the guardhouse, a little brick building to the left of the main villa. The others made for the rooms where the Trotskys and their grandson Seva were asleep. They fired murderously into these two rooms, aiming through windows and closed doors.

The bullets fired at the windows were in part deflected by the steel shutters, but when the police examined the bedroom they found no less than seventy-six impacted into the adobe wall and the floor.

Today, Seva is on the verge of old age, but he remains the orphaned child of Zinaida, Trotsky's daughter who was stripped of her Soviet nationality, and of Platon Volkov, lost in some hell. As a Mexican citizen, father of four beautiful young women, Seva is peaceably devoted to the indestructible memory of his grandfather. By profession a chemical engineer, he is the founder and curator of the moving museum, his childhood home in Coyoacán, where he lived with Trotsky's widow, Natalia Sedova. He recalls that night.

'I was sleeping peacefully in the room next to my grand-parents, when a noise woke me up. It was four thirty in the morning, and shortly after the rat-tat-tat of machine-gun fire began and went on for minutes on end. The whole house stank of gunpowder, like a battlefield. I was half-dreaming, but the danger was instant, and I felt instinctively what was going on. Then the guns fell silent and the attackers fled, throwing incendiary bombs in their wake. Soon after, every-thing was silent again.'

Natalia takes up the story:

'The door of the next room, where our grandson slept, opened on to a kind of furnace. On the threshold I caught a glimpse of a man in uniform who was twitching, surrounded by flames and shadows...His helmet, his distorted face and the metal buttons on his cape shone red. We remained crouch-ing together in a corner of the bedroom. I tried to move up a little more so that I could protect Leon Davidovitch because it looked as though the bullets were getting closer to him. We heard an anguished scream from Seva: "Grandfather!" The tone was both a warning and an appeal..."They've taken him", murmured Leon. The invasion of lights, shadows and gunfire lasted a long time and then stopped, making way for a deathly silence, a total, unbearable silence that petrified us'.[21]

May 1987. An old, etiolated pine, burned up by the pollution of modern day Mexico, finally dries out for good. Inside the house, in the shadow cast by the sun, there reigns a domestic simplicity in the wobbly furniture and in the small, everyday objects slowly gathering dust. The wall-plaster in the old man's bedroom is flaked and pocked with Stalinist bullet-holes.

This house has nothing of the sanctuary. Some pretty girls are working in the office. The dead man's table is covered with a sheet of transparent plastic, as it has been since the fatal day. The excellent library is a meeting-place for historians and young utopians. They understand that the way things go depends on accumulated knowledge, on the experience of others and on things heard and related. On the shelves stand books by Herzen, Tolstoy and Taine, Nietzsche, Ibsen and Schnitzler, Dos Passos, Langston Hughes, London, Malraux, Freud and Maurras, Henri Béraud and the admirable works of Victor Serge, Barbusse and Augustin Souchy's *Socialisme libertaire*. The margins of these books are covered in notes and comments. In one of them, a string of outraged exclamation marks has actually pierced the paper: Boris Souvarine's *Stalin*. About Ibsen there are a few notes on a blank page; 'The artist who negates is infinitely higher than the symbolist and the prophet.' Elsewhere, on a draft to André Breton: 'The fight for revolutionary ideas in art begins with the struggle for artistic truth, conceived not as obedience to one school or another, but as the inflexible loyalty of the artist to his inner self... Do not lie! That is the saving formula...'

In the peaceful garden, the spirit of place is at work. Numerous were the visitors who crossed the world to join the fight against Stalin. I am glad that the French weren't the last to do so either. The Rosmers, Jean van Heijenoort made haste, from Prinkipo to Barbizon, from Lagny-sur-Marne to Mexico. At the heart of tragedy, they enjoyed an enlightened rest in Coyoacán, that oasis protected from Thermidor's murderers.

The now elderly men I met have renounced nothing of what they were. They retain an overwhelming freshness. They haven't got rich and they haven't won honours, but they have remained possessed by the passion of their youth, some of them mad about science, others about art; they never disown the utopian dreams they had at twenty.

Maître Gérard Rosenthal, 'comrade Rosenthal', Trotsky's lawyer, is a charming old gentleman in retirement, his mind lucid. He recalls the tenth anniversary celebrations of the Moscow Revolution in 1927 as if they happened yesterday; he can still remember Trotsky on the telephone, when Bukharin informed him he had been expelled from the Party. Pierre Naville, one of Breton's associates at the birth of Surrealism, is also retired now, but still a forceful figure. With some emotion, he recalls the suicide-protest of the Bolshevik Joffé, and his body in the open coffin. 'With a little bloodied hole, right there, on the temple.' Later on, in the 1960s, Naville went to Havana with Michel Leiris, because then hopes were pinned on Cuba...

It was the Chief of the Mexican Secret Police, Colonel Sanchez Salazar, who headed the enquiry, helped by the highest police authorities in the federal district. Nevertheless the investigations dragged on for weeks. Little by little, even the members of the enquiry began to question the reality of the attack... Perhaps Trotsky and his disciples had mounted the pantomime themselves to gain publicity?... How otherwise could such an operation have missed its target? There were hundreds of bullet holes in all the walls of the house but no one was even wounded, unless one counts Seva, whose big toe was grazed...

A kind of delirium now gripped the Stalinist press, and on 3 May three young men who acted as Trotsky's bodyguard were arrested and interrogated about the fake attack mounted by Trotsky himself. President Cárdenas responded by immediately ordering their release.

On 1 June, at a press conference, Lev Davidovitch denounced Stalin and the GPU. *El Popular*, a pro-Communist daily put out by the CTM union, claimed that 'Trotsky is engaged in a battle of nerves against Mexico. The attack is an international blackmail!' Enrique Ramirez, one of the leaders of the Mexican Communist Party, was of the opinion that 'Trotsky had himself attacked, to make the Communists look like terrorists.' Despite the suspicions that he had begun to attract, the painter Siqueiros also published a declaration in which he poured

scorn on 'Trotsky's last practical joke, the work of a profes-
sional spy'.

But on 18 June the tissue of lies fell away. Thirty people
were arrested. The enquiry had followed the red thread all the
way back to the Communist schoolmaster Luis Martinez, who
had hired the police uniforms. Two women, Anita Martinez
and Julia Barradas de Serrano, were paid by Siqueiros's secretary to lie in wait and seduce the police watch in the little hut
near the main gateway to the villa. One of the women was
the wife of a veteran of the Spanish war, and a member of the
Stalinist Party politburo, David Serrano Andonegui. A Communist from the Canaries, Rosendo Gómez Lorenzo, was also
in on this, and it wasn't long before the accused denounced
the chief commando: none other than the painter David Alfaro
Siqueiros, helped by his collaborator Antonio Pujol.

Born in 1898, Siqueiros was editor of *El Machete*, the leading
Communist journal in Mexico; he was also a founder member
of the Mexican Communist Party, and a self-appointed lieuten-
ant-colonel in the Spanish Republican Army. Later on, this
international agent for the GPU was allowed to leave Mexico
unharmed, under the protection of the Stalinist poet Pablo
Neruda.

As for Sheldon Harte, the young American bodyguard, his
mutilated body was found on 25 June, at the bottom of a pit
of quicklime, near the village of Tlalminalco, in a maisonette
rented by Siqueiros' brothers-in-law, Luis and Leopoldo
Arenal.

Lev Davidovitch was forced nevertheless to confront the
accusations in the Mexican press and the fabulations of the
Stalinists. The latter claimed that Comrade Siqueiros was 'half-
mad', 'an irresponsible adventurer' who had sold himself once
and for all to Trotsky, the latter having paid him to set up the
simulated attack...

Four days after the attack, on 28 May 1940, Trotsky was to
meet his future murderer for the first time.

Alfred Rosmer, a founding member of the French Communist

Party, was a morally exigent man, steeped in political science. He was very soon expelled from the Party. When Trotsky was in Paris, before the First World War, he made friends with Rosmer. During the civil war, the latter went with him to the Soviet Union and became his constant companion, in the Kremlin and in his armoured carriage. Later, he was one of Trotsky's closest collaborators in Prinkipo, when the international opposition against Stalin began to take shape. Marguerite and Alfred Rosmer had come to Mexico to bring little Seva, orphan of Zina and Platon, home to his grandparents.

The Rosmers, who had only a few weeks left in Mexico, had showed great affection for a young Belgian, Jacson Mornard . . .

Sylvia Agelof, a woman of Russian origin, and a militant in the American Leftist Opposition, had met this seductive young man on her way to Paris in June 1938. At his instigation, Sylvia was manipulated by an American friend, Ruby Weil, in league with the Soviet special services. It was she who organized their meeting, at which the young Belgian introduced himself as the son of a diplomat. He was a good-looking boy, elegant, debonair, with a taste for sporting journalism: Jacson Mornard. Later on, he persuaded Sylvia to go with him to Mexico . . .

Sylvia is now middle-aged, having long since rebuilt her life, exorcizing the momentous historical plot to which she fell victim. Formerly seduced and betrayed, she now leads a tranquil, bourgeois existence in New York, which I chose not to intrude upon. Maria Craipeau-Blunden, a friend of Sylvia's at that period in Paris, provides us with a witness, however. Maria is a woman of great vivacity, a sharp-eyed intellectual who for many years after the Second World War was New York correspondent for *Franc-Tireur*, originally a Resistance journal. Maria, who was 'adopted' by the Third International, left her native Poland at the age of fourteen and arrived in Paris with only a bundle of clothes in 1931. She was a daughter of the Revolution. In 1933, when Hitler came to power as Chancellor of the Reich, this young Communist demanded an explanation from her organization of the political line taken by the German Communist Party, known as that of the Third Period, which led to disaster. Totally bewildered, having failed to

47

obtain a satisfying answer, she happened to hear, almost by chance, a speech by Pierre Naville. Surprised by the political lucidity of the Leftist Opposition, she rallied to Trotsky's banner.

If the proletarians had no homeland, revolutionaries make one big family. When Sylvia Agelof arrived in Paris, it was Maria who befriended her and taught her the rudiments of French. It was also to Maria that, one day, Sylvia introduced the young man she had fallen in love with, Jacson Mornard.

'He was a rather bland, pleasant, elegant fellow, who fitted in socially everywhere. He spoke of his father's numerous diplomatic postings, of his mother whom he adored and who was a great horsewoman. Jac wasn't interested in anything much, least of all in politics. When we came to talk to Sylvia, he would leave the room. He was sweet, generous, charming. An inoffensive type. Later, when Sylvia tired of Paris and wanted to return to New York and to her job, she hesitated a bit because of Jac. It was then, as if on the spur of the moment, that he suggested she translate articles on psychology from English into French for an agency; and I was to help Sylvia type them up. We received good money for this. Then one day at work, I stopped, my fingers still on the keyboard and turned to Sylvia: "Listen Sylvia, there's something wrong with this; this kind of job doesn't usually pay so well." We sat down on the bed, started smoking as usual, and chatted about it. He wasn't interested in politics...Didn't participate in our discussions...So? We thought he was just madly in love, and didn't want to lose her, and put it down to that.'

That 28 May 1940, in Mexico, Jacson Mornard parked his car and went through the portico into the garden at Coyoacán at seven fifty-eight in the morning. He had offered to drive the Rosmers to the port of Vera Cruz where they would embark for Europe. The charming Jacson owned a big Buick, and he too had to go to the Atlantic port for his work. A happy coincidence, and the Rosmers would be spared the train journey of four hundred and fifty kilometres linking Mexico to the coast. They accepted his invitation. Natalia, exhausted by recent events, decided to seize the heaven-sent opportunity and join the party, accompanied by Reba Hansen, wife of Trotsky's first secretary. In the garden, amid the commotion of departure, Trotsky and the Rosmers bade each other fond farewells. The car was loaded up and Jacson, whom they surprised inside the house, explained he had just been showing Seva how to operate a model glider he had given him.

In the crowded streets of Vera Cruz, Jacson drew up outside a building and asked a passerby the way to the port. Natalia took note of this, remembering that the Belgian had always said he visited the city twice a month for his work...But she soon forgot about it. Who can live in a state of perpetual suspicion?

Every morning after the commando raid, Natalia confided, Trotsky rejoiced at his escape. He was the only major 'criminal' who was still alive and out of Stalin's reach. His American collaborators insisted that he leave Mexico where he was too easy a target for the GPU. George Novack was especially of this opinion. But Trotsky replied:

'I know I am condemned. I am a soldier and I can see that all the cards are stacked against me. Stalin is enthroned in Moscow with more power and resources at his disposal than any of the tsars. I am alone with a few friends and almost no resources, against a powerful killing-machine which has already eliminated the other opponents, Lenin's associates in the Politburo and the Soviet government. So what can I do?'[22]

Measures were nevertheless taken to protect the Coyoacán house more efficiently. A campaign in America raised several thousand dollars, and the villa was transformed into a fortress. Walls six metres high were built round the house, along with a bomb-proof redoubt with floors and walls of reinforced concrete. Electrically controlled steel doors replaced the old wooden portico that gave on to the Calle Viena. Three new brick turrets were erected to overlook the garden and adjacent streets. Construction workers installed barriers of barbed wire and flexible mesh designed to withstand hand-bomb and grenade attacks. The Mexican government tripled the number of policemen on guard outside the villa, and James Cannon, one of the leaders of the American Leftist Opposition, went to Minneapolis to recruit some good bodyguard material from the Truckers Union...

On Thursday 8 August, Jacson and Sylvia went to have tea with the Trotskys. It was the first time the couple had been invited to Coyoacán. Little by little, Sylvia Agelof's 'husband' got closer to the old revolutionary.

On the morning of 20 August 1940, Natalia noticed that Trotsky had begun the day in excellent spirits. A double dose of pills had helped him sleep soundly. As usual, he busied himself with his rabbits and plants. That afternoon, he had planned to dictate an article on the American mobilization. After lunch, Natalia opened the door of his office, and found him in his usual attitude, pen in hand, poring over his files and newspaper cuttings. 'I was glad that he felt so well, because for some time he had complained of tiresome weakness...I felt he was living in a self-imposed prison, like a cloistered monk, but dedicated to a great struggle...At about five o'clock we had tea'.[23]

Twenty minutes later, Natalia Ivanovna saw Trotsky near the rabbit hutches, with a man who held a hat and had a raincoat on his arm – the August sky is often heavy in Mexico. It was Jacson Mornard. The pretext for his visit: Jacson, who had to go to New York for a few days, wanted to read Trotsky his first article, on Max Schachtman's theory of the 'Third Camp', which opposed that of the Trotskyists. The old man invited his visitor to follow him into his office. Trotsky sat down in his armchair in front of the huge table covered with reviews and books. In a pen tray was a paper-knife, a lorgnette and some cartridge cases from commando Siqueiros' machine-gun. There was an old fashioned blotter, the dictaphone with its recording rolls, and, a few centimetres from Trotsky's hand, a ·25 automatic. In the desk drawer there was a colt ·38. The two weapons were loaded, six bullets in the magazine. The security alarm bell was also within reach. As Trotsky bent over the article to begin reading it, Jacson Mornard put his raincoat down on the table. A few seconds later Natalia, in the office, heard a terrible cry of pain and surprise. Joseph Hansen, Trotsky's secretary, who was in one of the watch towers, also heard that long drawn out, terrible groan of anguish, something between a cry and a sob. Sounds of a scuffle came from the study while in the garden below, Melquiades, one of the Mexican guards, aimed his gun at the lower window. He saw Trotsky, wearing his blue twill jacket, in hand-to-hand combat with Jacson.

When Lev Davidovitch had started to read, his attention fully on the text, Mornard, taking the ice-pick out of his rolled-up raincoat, had struck him a blow that penetrated seven centimetres into the victim's skull, reaching vital parts of the brain.

May 1987. Esteban Volkov, the little Seva of the story, is seated in the garden at Coyoacán, in the shade of some purple bougainvillaeas. One feels the effort it must be for this solid man to relate yet again the events of the 20 August 1940.

'I was coming calmly home from school, walking through the quiet district which was then the frame of my existence. Approaching the house, I was seized by an instinctive fear. A feeling of anguish . . . Something abnormal was happening. In front of the entrance were groups of men, and cars parked in a hurry. I quickened my step, and then I saw the shocked faces. Jacson, Sylvia's husband, was in the middle of the garden, held by police officers. He was dishevelled, his face unrecognizable; a man disfigured, groaning and sobbing . . . I had never seen a man in such a state. I understood nothing. When I went into the library, I saw Lev Davidovitch wounded, lying on the ground, but the guards and others stopped me from going any closer. My grandfather had said: "Don't let Seva in, the child mustn't see this." Later, he crossed the garden for the last time, on a stretcher carried by male nurses.'

Still conscious, Trotsky whispered in English to Joe Hansen, raising his hand to his heart: 'It's the end . . . This time . . . they've succeeded . . .'

Natalia: 'A Green-Cross ambulance drove towards the town

and then through it. The lights were already burning. The siren wailed incessantly. Leon Davidovitch's left arm was paralysed, while his right arm kept making circles in the air... "How do you feel?" "Better... Better", he answered me. At the Green-Cross Hospital, the stretcher had to get through a crowd of onlookers. I was trembling. They could strike again right here... A nurse began to cut his strands of grey hair. Leon Davidovitch smiled at me and whispered "And here's the barber..." Because, during the day, we had talked of getting one... Then he called Joe Hansen over and dictated some words that Joe wrote in a notebook. "What did he dictate to you?" I asked our comrade. "Something about French statistics." It was strange...

'The nurses cut away his clothes. Suddenly he said, distinctly, in a solemn, very sad tone: "I don't want others to undress me... I want you to do it." Those were his last words to me. I undressed him. I put my lips to his. He returned my kiss, once, and then once more. Then he lost consciousness. I stayed all night by his bedside, waiting for him to come round, back to life. His eyes were closed and his breathing at times difficult, at others smooth. The night and the next day passed like this. Towards evening, after the trepanning, the doctors noted an improvement. Then his breathing became short and harsh... He was lifted up with his head slumped on to his shoulder, but his features were still proud. I hoped against all hope. So often, during our life together, I had seen him overcome crises, and escape unharmed from danger, holding on when it seemed superhuman to do so, and I still believed in the impossible. He was going to recover his usual vigour, open his eyes and decide to go on living...

'I collapsed, exhausted, into a chair. A presentiment, perhaps a movement, awakened me. I saw two doctors in white coats in front of me. I understood... Leon Davidovitch had died calmly, an instant earlier, on 21 August 1940, at seven twenty-five in the evening. He was sixty years old'.[24]

The President of Mexico, Lázaro Cárdenas, made a violent attack on the Mexican Communist Party, on 30 August: 'The communists are in league with a foreign power in organizing armed attacks that dishonour civilization. The result is the recent crime for which history will forever brand those who planned it with dishonour and those who perpetrated it with infamy.'

On 17 April 1943, two years and eight months after the murder, Jacson Mornard appeared before a Mexican court to be sentenced. He was condemned to nineteen and a half years imprisonment, and to a further six months for carrying an illegal weapon. A few years later, Julián Gorkin unmasked Jacson's real identity. He was called Ramón Mercader. Nearly twenty years later, after his release, he was awarded the Order of Lenin in Moscow...

Trotsky's funeral prompted immense popular sympathy in Mexico. Three hundred thousand Mexicans, from every corner of the republic, walked the streets, often barefoot, following the procession from the funeral parlour to the cremation room in the cemetery.

Nationalist Mexico, having been expropriated by the great petrol companies, fell victim to the joint aggression of Great Britain and the United States. These brutal attacks from without, and the murder of Trotsky by the Soviet Union under Stalin, were felt to be part of a conspiracy by the great nations of the North against the Mexican Revolution. The people were demonstrating against this coalition. They didn't really know who Trotsky was, he was simply one of the great generals in the greatest revolution of the century; in some ways he resembled the Mexican generals of the great Mexican Revolution. He was a symbol.

May 1987. The rabbit hutches which had collapsed in the Coyoacán garden have today been rebuilt. The house, now a museum of the federal district of Mexico, has just been restored by the Mexican authorities. The ashes of Leon Trotsky, mixed with those of Natalia, repose in a sealed urn, behind a monument in concrete engraved with the hammer and sickle. It was made by the workers of the Builders Union. Yuccas climb the column.

Some young American couples with their children have gathered round the monument. The little ones play. Not far from the group, against a pillar of the out-house for the car, a plaque of old marble reads: '*In memory of Robert Sheldon Harte, 1915-1940. Murdered by Stalin.*'

Trotsky left a document in an envelope. His will.

'My high blood pressure (which is still rising) deceives those near me as to my real state of health. I am active and capable of working, but the end is evidently near. These lines will be made public after my death[...]. I thank all those friends who have remained loyal to me throughout the hardest years of my life. I shall not name any in particular, because I cannot name them all.

'However, I think I am justified in making an exception for my companion, Natalia Ivanovna Sedova. In addition to the happiness of being a fighter for the Socialist cause, destiny gave me the happiness of being her husband. During nearly forty years of our life together, she has remained an inexhaustible source of love, magnanimity and tenderness. She has undergone great suffering, especially in the last phase of our life. But I draw some comfort from the fact that she has also known days of happiness.

'For forty-three years of my thinking life I have been a revolutionary; for forty-two of those years I fought under the banner of Marxism. If I had to start all over again, I would of course try to avoid this or that error, but the general course of my life would remain unchanged[...]

'Natasha has just come up to the window from the courtyard and opened it wider so that air can circulate more freely in my room. I can see a wide strip of green grass along the wall, the pale blue sky above, and sunlight on everything. Life is beautiful. May the future generations cleanse it of all evil, oppression and violence, and enjoy it to the full.'[25]

Notes

1 *Correspondance Léon et Natalia Trotsky, 1933-1938*, Coll. 'Témoins', Gallimard.
2 *Vie et mort de Trotsky*, Victor Serge, Aimot-Dumont.
3 *Sept ans auprès de Trotsky, De Prinkipo à Coyoacán*, Jean van Heijenoort, Lettre nouvelles-Maurice Nadeau.
4 *Correspondance*, op. cit.
5 Victor Serge, op. cit.
6 *Trotsky*, biography by Pierre Broué, Fayard, 1990.
7 ibid.
8 Jean van Heijenoort, op. cit.
9 Pierre Broué, op. cit.
10 'Prolégomènes à un troisième manifeste du surréalisme ou non', in André Breton, *Manifestes*, 1942.
11 In *Cahiers Léon Trotsky*, no.25 March 1986, Grenoble.
12 Ibid.
13 *L'Art et la Révolution*, Léon Trotsky, *Oeuvres.*, E.D.I.
14 *Cahiers Léon Trotsky*, op. cit.
15 Ibid.
16 André Breton, op. cit.
17 André Breton to Leon Trotsky, 9 August 1938, Houghton Library, no.369.
18 Victor Serge, op. cit.
19 *Journal d'exil*, Léon Trotsky, Folio, Gallimard.
20 Pierre Broué, op. cit.
21 Victor Serge, op. cit.
22 Ibid.
23 Ibid.
24 Ibid.
27 Léon Trotsky, op. cit.

The testimony of Leon Trotsky's immediate family and his contemporaries in this text was recorded by the author in 1987 and 1988.

A Portrait of Leon Trotsky
James T. Farrell

The life of Leon Trotsky is one of the great tragic dramas of modern history. Pitting his brain and will against the despotic rulers of a great empire, fully conscious of the power, the resources, the cunning and cruelty of his enemy, Trotsky had one weapon at his command – his ideas. His courage never faltered; his will never broke. His children were murdered or driven to suicide; his friends, his co-workers and secretaries were killed. His entire generation was annihilated. He lived the life of a prisoner, continually exposed to the blow of an assassin. He was fatalistic enough to know that he would probably not live to see his ideas triumph. Nevertheless, he accepted without a moment's hesitation all the risks involved in the propagation of his doctrines. Finally, unable to refute his ideas, they drove a pickaxe into his brain.

During the last forty years Leon Trotsky's life was consecrated to one end – the socialist revolution. It was with the greatest of contempt that he looked upon the men in power who had traded their historic roles for portfolios. And how did their conduct compare with his when they too lost power and were forced into exile? Nomadic statesmen, they travelled from capital to capital begging favours from bourgeois public opinion, intriguing, manoeuvering, manipulating, with the hope that perhaps the Quai d'Orsay, Downing Street, or the White House might restore their portfolios. But Trotsky was big enough to stand alone, always rising to the level of his historic position. In exile he produced book after book, a brilliant series of works unmatched in our time that, even more than the example of his life, remain the legacy of future generations. And you cannot drive a pickaxe into ideas.

I admired Trotsky as an historical figure, and Trotsky the man inspired me with affection. Even his critics have recognized Trotsky's brilliance as a writer; but his work is more than brilliant – it is fertile, suggestive, illuminating. Compared to its method, acuteness and high seriousness, the productions of our American political scientists and journalists seem morally flabby, spineless, full of facile improvisations. No political writer alive today can rival his record of almost clairvoyant predictions of later events.

Most of Trotsky's critics have presented him as a modern Machiavelli, hungry for personal power, who even in exile was desperately seeking to recapture it. This conception of Trotsky as a power-hungry Machiavellian falsifies his life. Trotsky, the materialist, took ideas with the greatest seriousness. He defended Marxism dogmatically. He defended dialectical materialism at times when neither its defence nor its rejection involved questions of power. His policies were based on his ideas. His decisions were in harmony with his premises and his principles. It is noteworthy that anecdotes about Trotsky, reminiscences of personal discussions, and his letters do not contain a single cynical statement about the methods necessary to attain power which one inevitably finds in the records of genuine Machiavellians like Napoleon. He had supreme confidence in the validity of his ideas. To hold to the conception of Trotsky as a Machiavellian, one must argue that almost his entire life, his voluminous books and his numberless letters were all a false front to mask a secret motive which he hid from his closest friends and collaborators.

For Trotsky, all intellectual questions were practical and concrete. His test for the validity of ideas was how they worked out in practice, in the actual framework of history. In this respect, he was close to the pragmatists. While Trotsky upheld some dogmas and was sometimes even schematic in his thinking, he was a relativist in the handling of ideas. He had an acute sense of the involvement of events in each other, of their inter-relationships. I recall how, during the course of a disagreement with him, he emphasized the necessity of conceiving a fact not merely as something which exists but also as something which is in process of becoming. This sense of becoming in events, of the relational character of events to each other was one of his most remarkable intellectual traits. He never isolated political events; he saw them consistently in their international setting. He was no crude empiricist, nor did he indulge in easy psychological interpretations as a substitute for objective analysis. Some of us thought that our general theories were at times more sound than Trotsky's. We even took delight in proofs that his philosophical formulations were not modern and could easily be refuted through logical analysis. Yet Trotsky was more creative with his bad epistemology than we were with our good epistemology.

Trotsky was a harsh opponent, never hesitating to break with friend after friend on issues of principle and policy. In this regard he did not differ from most men of strong convictions. In his thinking he was more inclined to draw sharp distinctions than to conciliate differences. These temperamental traits were, in a sense, psychological adaptations to his chosen way of life. Moreover, a man less intransigent than he could not have endured the blows he received in his days of exile. In public, Trotsky was often sharp, alert, metallic. Under questioning he was guarded and suspicious, inclined to break out in sharp invective or ironic statements. But his adamant side did not exhaust his personality. Many of his friends and disciples knew him as a warm and generous man. I think he wanted friends and tended to be excessively trusting with them, so much so that he often regarded people whom he had met only a few times as friends. In his personal relations he was simple and charming – a man of singular grace.

Highly disciplined, Trotsky was unsparing of himself, subordinating all his impulses to his central purpose. I have never known another man whose very organism was so completely under the control of his will and intelligence. What he hated most of all was stupidity. In fact, he so hated it that he could not even listen to stories about the stupidity of his enemies. He was also impatient of incompetence. I recall how on a picnic Trotsky watched a friend try to start a fire clumsily. This friend had broken with him politically. In a bantering way Trotsky suggested that his friend's politics matched his ability to start a fire. Finally he made the fire himself, quickly and efficiently.

One of Trotsky's traits that I admired most was his capacity for contempt. He knew how to despise those liberal intellectuals who, behind a set of pretentious gestures, invariably reflected the hypocrisy of bourgeois public opinion. At the same time such people puzzled him. A New York editor, who had printed attacks on Trotsky which virtually called him an assassin, requested to see him while vacationing in Mexico. He refused the request. But he was no snob. While intolerant of people who wished to visit him purely for curiosity's sake, he was hospitable to more serious visitors, regardless of their reputations or achievements. Thus he devoted as much care and thought to a letter to an unknown worker as he would to an article directed against a famous figure. He saw in everyone the representative of a class or of a social group, and in everyone's ideas he perceived their political consequences. His estimates of character, despite the charges of his critics, were generally not personal: they were political and intellectual. His brilliant character vignettes in *The History of the Russian Revolution* are actually social studies in miniature. In answering questions put to him by the Dewey Commission, he was most balanced in his evaluation of Stalin. He pointed out that Stalin did not become what he is today all at once, and at one time even Stalin was a good revolutionary. But to Lenin Trotsky had a personal relation. Even more than Marx, Lenin was (I think) his teacher. I would categorically discount the charge that Trotsky was really jealous of Lenin and used his memory to justify himself. On the contrary, his attitude to Lenin was one of reverence.

Some have been disconcerted by Trotsky's optimism and faith. But this faith, even if one cannot share it, is easily understood when one considers that they are necessary elements in any practical activity. What was to him a series of practical issues, was to his intellectualistic critics purely a set of formal questions. In formal intellectual activity we are not optimistic and believing but sceptical; and in some of Trotsky's theoretical opponents this scepticism sometimes results in irresponsibility.

While he was risking his life for his ideas, they are risking a syllogism.

Neither Stalinism nor the capitalist world can forgive Leon Trotsky. They will hate his memory, but they will never succeed in erasing it. History will know how to preserve it.

One of the best tributes we can pay Trotsky is to understand him. These notes are an effort toward such an understanding. I offer them in tribute to the memory of the Old Man.

Partisan Review, October 1940

The Mexican Album

Photo Credits

From the collection of Josep Maria Oliveras, Spain:
pages 6, 8, 56, 65 (above), 67, 69 (above), 71 (above), 72 (above), 74 (above), 76, 77, 78 (above), 79, 81, 82 (right), 85, 86 (right), 103, 104 (below), 105-107, 108 (below), 110 (top left; right), 112 (bottom left; right), 113, 114 (bottom), 115 (above), 116 (top right; below), 117-119, 120 (below), 121 (top right; below), 122.

From the Archives of the Institut Léon Trotsky:
pages 65 (below), 66, 68, 69 (below), 70, 71 (below), 72 (below), 73, 74 (below), 75, 78 (below), 80, 82 (left), 83, 84, 86 (left), 87-102, 104 (above), 108 (above), 109, 110 (bottom left), 111, 112 (top left), 114 (top, middle), 115 (below), 116 (top left), 120 (above), 121 (top left).

At Coyoacán, Trotsky at
work helped by his
Russian secretary, Rae
Spiegel.

above: Family reunion in Mexico – Trotsky is flanked by Frida Kahlo and Natalia,
Rivera sits on the left.
opposite: The table decorated by Rivera for Trotsky's 60th birthday.

Above: Cinema was an event at Coyoacán. Seva is in the front row.
Below: Natalia Ivanovna and Marguerite Rosmer.

Some Mexican friends.
The Fernandez couple
belonged to the Left
Opposition.

Jean van Heijenoort, who organized everything.

74

Above: Front row – Natalia, Frida and Cristina Kahlo, Ruth Agelof. Behind – Trotsky, Costa Amic, Martinez and David Rey (Daniel Rebull).
Opposite: Trotsky and Alfred Rosmer.

Above: Trotsky and
Natalia with Diego
Rivera.
Below: With Otto Rühle,
who had voted with
Liebknecht in the
Reichstag against war in
1914-15. He took refuge
in Mexico.

Left: Costa Amic, Trotsky, Martinez and the POUM veteran David Rey.
Right: Trotsky with Rivera and Cristina Kahlo.

Natalia with Albert Glotzer, shorthand secretary for the Commission of Enquiry.

Above: Facing the Commission of Enquiry, with Jean van Heijenoort.
Below: John Dewey, chairman of the Commission, with Otto Rühle.

Trotsky the Mexican – he liked white suits, and a peasant hat.

otsky's preferred writing method was to create a patchwork of typed text,
ndwritten notes and translations.

Above: Lyova Sedov, the 'Kid' as the GPU dubbed him; walking with his partner, Jeanne Martin, in Paris.
Opposite: Seva in Marseilles with Jean van Heijenoort, 1932.

Seva with his grandparents in Mexico, late 1939.

...monstration of deportees on 7 November 1928: 'Down with the Kulak, the NEPman
...d the bureaucrat', 'Long live the dictatorship of the proletariat'.

ПРАВО СИДЯТ: Валентинов, Тамаркин, Яновлев, Климентьев
СТОЯТ: Эльцин, Гендельман.

Despite Stalin's efforts to cut off communication, Trotsky received photographs smuggled out of the USSR. Under this one, taken before deportation to Ust-Vym, Trotsky's handwriting identifie (from left to right, seated) Valentinov, Yakolev, the Moscow worker Klementiev, (standing) V.B. Yeltsin, Trotsky's secretary, and Gendelman.

this group of deportees there are two of Trotsky's close colleagues:
p left, V.B. Yeltsin and middle right, I.M. Poznansky.

91

Above: The poet, the painter and the revolutionary.
Below: Trotsky with André Breton at Coyoacán.

92

A Léon Trotsky
en souvenir des jours
passés dans sa lumière,
avec mon admiration
et mon dévouement
absolus
André Breton
Mexico
20 juillet
1938.

From left to right:
Rivera, Frida Kahlo,
Natalia, Reba Hansen,
Breton, and last on
the right, Jean van
Heijenoort, known as
'Van'.

Opposite: On the steps of the Teotihuacán Pyrami

eep-sea fishing off Vera Cruz.

After gathering his favourite cactus, the *viejitos*.

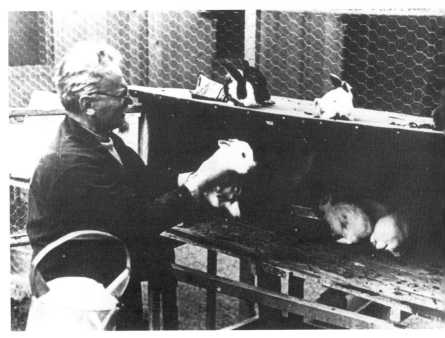

Trotsky's rabbits added variety to the household diet.

Above: The house in Coyoacán after construction of the keep, calle Viena.
Below: Two of Trotsky's bodyguards.

103

Above: The guard with Corporal Casas.
Below: In front of the outer wooden gateway in Coyoacán.

104

nvestigators discover incendiary bombs and a rope-ladder used during the Siqueiros raid.
onth later, the corpse of Robert Sheldon Harte was found in a pit near Tlalminalco.

ve: After his arrest, David Alfaro Siqueiros at a press conference.
w: Siqueiros with his friends from the State of Jalisco who hid him.

107

After the attack, Trotsky was called upon to exculpate himself: the Stalinist press accused him of setting it up. Here he is signing the record of his interrogation.

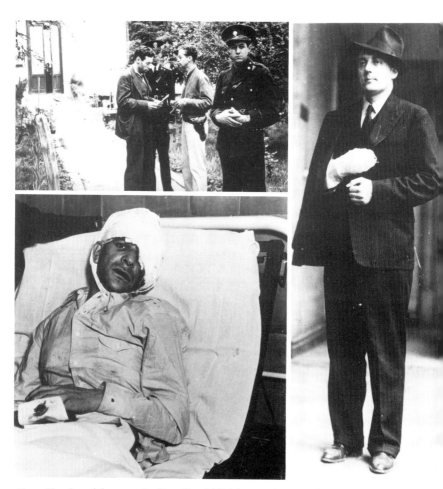

Above: The day of the assassination; Harold Robins, an American bodyguard, is on the right
Below: Ramón Mercader after his arrest, having been attacked by Trotsky's bodyguards.
Right: Jo Hansen, Trotsky's bodyguard, wounded in the struggle.

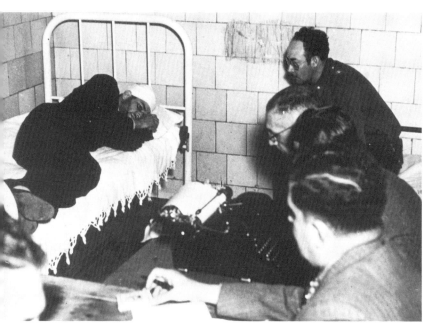

interrogation of Mercader.

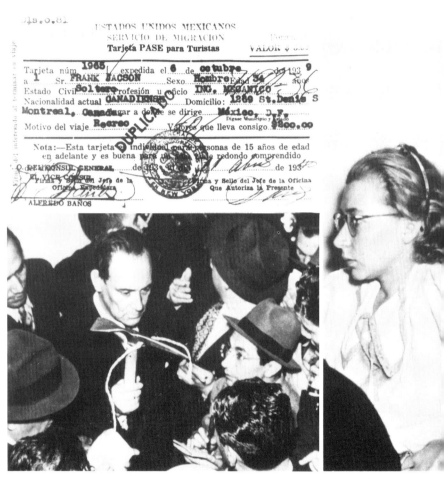

Above: All Mercader's weapons: the visa with false identity, the ice-pick, and Sylvia Agelof, whom he used to get close to Trotsky.
Opposite: (above) Mercader in front of the presiding magistrate; (below) the central man in the pale suit is the deputy head of the Mexican security police, Jesús Galindo.

112

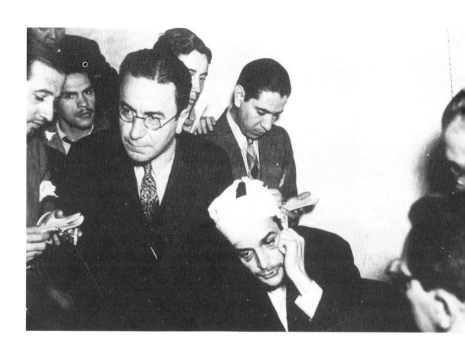

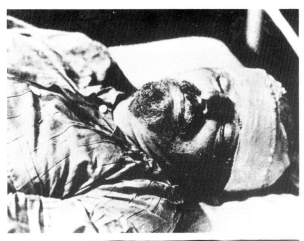

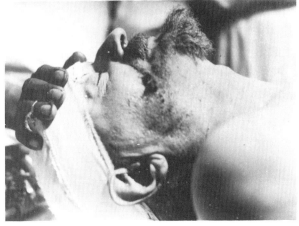

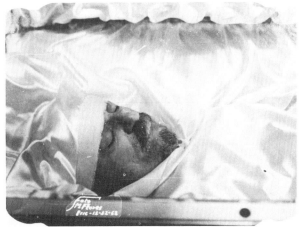

114

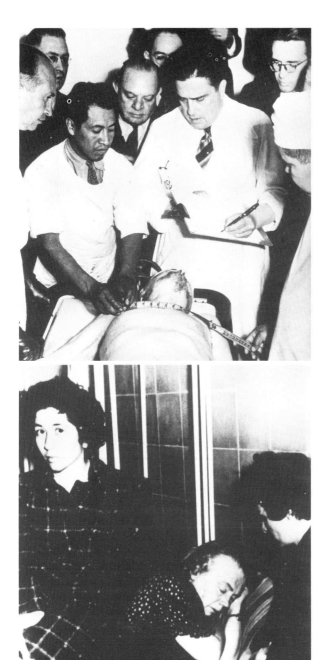

Below: Natalia Ivanovna in the care of Myra Ward and Evelyn Reed.

Above: Mexican militants mount guard over the bier.
Below: The Cárdenas government is represented by Mexican officers as Trotsky lies in state.
Opposite: Natalia Ivanovna's last sight of her husband; thousands of Mexicans follow the hearse on 22 August.

116

Above: The coffin for cremation.
Below: Trotsky's ashes, which now rest in the garden at Coyoacán beside those of Natalia, who died in Paris in 1962.

In August 1941, Natalia wrote to President Cárdenas
to say she had been threatened by Stalinist killers.

Above: Caridad Mercader, Ramón's mother, parades at the head of PSUC militiamen in Barcelona in 1936.
Below: Mercader, dressed in civilian clothes, during his detention.

México, D.F., a 23 de marzo de 1960

Al C Licenciado
D. Gustavo Díaz Ordaz.
Secretario de Gobernación,
Presente.

El suscrito, Jacques Mornard, de
nacionalidad checoeslovaca, recluido en la Peni-
tenciaría del D.F., manifiesta a usted, con todo
respeto, que no tiene ningún inconveniente en ser
entregado a las autoridades diplomáticas de Che-
coeslovaquia, al ser puesto en libertad, pues este
país le ha brindado su asilo.

Respetuosamente
J. Mornard.

above: (left) Mercader in his Mexican cell; (right) on his release after twenty years' detention.
below: Still using the name 'Mornard', he applies for entry into Czechoslovakia, and flies there
on his release. In Moscow he was awarded the Lenin Prize.

121

Afterword
Pierre Broué

Trotsky, the man whose final exile Alain Dugrand has depicted, with the help of photographs, in the foregoing text, has not become a subject of indifference at this late phase of the twentieth century – a century Trotsky himself welcomed in from a prison cell. Writer and journalist, formidable orator and political leader, army chief and literary critic, Trotsky continues to provoke debate and arouse passions nearly half a century after his violent death.

By the time of his deportation and his collaboration with the *Eastern Observer*, at the beginning of the 1905 revolution, he was already a well-known publicist who had had violent quarrels and made several enemies. When he got to Europe in 1903, an associate of Plekhanov and Lenin in *Iskra*, [the *Spark* group], he very soon became the *bête noire* of the former, and abandoned the latter in the middle of the 1903 schism, to rally the Mensheviks. Favouring the reunification of the Party, in 1904 he managed the considerable feat of finding himself alienated from the Bolsheviks and rejected by the Mensheviks.

Nevertheless, his qualities as a Tribune of the People, as much as his clearsightedness and determination earned him the position, at twenty-six years old, of spokesman for the Workers of St Petersburg; he later became president of their soviet. Under arrest, he delivered himself of an anti-Tsarist indictment in front of his judges, a cry of optimism and revolutionary faith. Imprisoned, he effected a dramatic escape which he described in a kind of popular 'best-seller'.

Once in the West, he began his life as a journalist and militant, reading, writing, travelling. He attended the International Socialist Congresses, came to know all the eminent leaders of the International, travelled the warring Balkans and reviewed Viennese exhibitions. Having learned the lesson of 1905, he was simultaneously developing his theory of 'permanent revolution' and realized that the proletariat would have to take power in Russia to fulfil the tasks of the bourgeois revolution, which would in turn open the way to the European revolution.

The war pushed Trotsky the free-shooter further to the left; until then he had been more of a centrist in debate. He ran a Russian Internationalist daily in Paris and reported on the Manifesto of the Internationalist Conference at Zimmerwald. Very quickly, he emerged as one of the most eminent socialists in the Internationalist group in France among those who refused the idea that socialism should be limited to one country. Expelled to Spain, and from there to the United States, he became a militant on the left wing of the Socialist Party, waging war in the New World – where he proclaimed the Apocalypse – against the old guard of war-time socialists.

As the only revolutionary really known because of his activities in 1905, and with his talent for writing and oratory, it was he who rallied the Bolshevik Party, fighting for the power of the soviets, shortly after his return to Russia in March 1917. It was thus that he rejoined Lenin, from whom he had been separated for so long. From now on their two names were indissolubly linked. The October Revolution: Lenin and Trotsky.

As President of the Petrograd Soviet, and then of the Revolutionary Military Committee, he organized and led the October Rising which triumphed the day of his thirty-eighth birthday.

Commissar of the People for Foreign Affairs, and then, in 1918, for War, he became head of a new army, the Red Army made up of workers and peasants, which he conceived, inspired and led. A member of the Central Committee and the Politburo, and respected leader of the Communist International, he twice opposed Lenin, first in 1918 over the Brest-Litovsk treaty, then in 1920 over the 'militarization' of the Unions that he advocated in his rigorous 'War Communism' policy. But this did not cloud the trust that existed between the two men, manifest particularly in the last months of Lenin's life, when the latter depended on him in his struggle against Stalin.

Let no one be mistaken. For all those who concentrated their hatred and frustrations on the Soviet Union and the Revolution, Trotsky is the one who 'stabbed the Allies in the back', who 'compromised with the Boche', and who 'swindled' the small investors by refusing to honour Russian loans. Their hatred is mixed with anti-Semitism, as the caricatures make clear. For the Soviets and the Communists, on the other hand, he is the 'organizer of victory', second only to Lenin, if not his equal.

This black-and-white image did not last. Certainly, the hatred emanating from the Old World remained intense; Churchill as much as Hitler set on him and his followers right up to the end. But in the USSR itself, the picture altered radically after the death of Lenin. Convinced that Trotsky was a menace to their power, his successors set about destroying his heroic image and rewriting history.

The Zinoviev-Kamenev-Stalin triumvirate, which confronted Trotsky during the debate on currency reform in 1923, proceeded with prudence: the assemblies reacted badly to attacks on Trotsky. For a while, they contented themselves with identifying the triumvirate with the 'Old Bolsheviks' and with what they called 'Leninism'. It was thus, in counterpoint, that the concept of 'Trotskyism' appeared, with its anti-Leninist connotation; it was finally cast as Menshevik in inspiration!

It was Bukharin who first made use of the disagreements between Lenin and Trotsky recorded between 1917 and 1923; he brought up the debates over the Brest Litovsk treaty and the 'militarized' unions. The ground was thus prepared for the 13th Party Congress in January 1924, at which Stalin accused Trotsky of harbouring 'Anarcho-Menshevik' ideas and of breaking with the 'Bolshevik Organization Line'. The final resolution accused the Opposition of revising Bolshevism and breaking with Leninism, but also branded it as 'petit-bourgeois deviationism'. Lenin's death strengthened the position of the triumvirate: misled by Stalin, Trotsky was absent from his solemn state funeral.

The pretext for the second offensive against him was provided by 'The Lessons of October' published in November 1924. His adversaries didn't deny that he had written – as Kamenev recognized – some of the most 'glorious pages' of Party history. But with the help of some of Lenin's words taken out of context, they accused him of having been 'a Menshevik agent in the working class from 1904-1917'. They claimed that Trotsky had not joined the Party repenting of his errors, but rather to recruit Lenin for Trotskyism when he pronounced himself in favour of 'power to the soviets'.

Trotsky was accused of 'undervaluing the peasantry' and advocating 'the dictatorship of industry'. Stalin contested his role in the October Rising, alluding to the existence of a 'centre' which in fact never functioned. But he struck him a serious blow when he published a letter to Tchkheidze, dated 1913: in it Trotsky claimed that 'Leninism' was based on lies and falsification, as Lenin systematically exploited all the backward elements of the Russian Workers Movement.

'Trotskyism' old and new, as defined by Stalin, was from then on characterized as the theory of permanent revolution which left out of account the poor peasants, refused the monolithic Bolshevik structure, and aimed at 'dethroning' Lenin.

The result of this 'literary debate' – the name given to this savage campaign – was Trotsky's departure from the government and his isolation in the Politburo, where the other members excluded him from the decision-making process.

Trotsky did not defend himself. He did not question the use of the term 'Leninism' against 'Trotskyism', and indeed against Lenin's thought itself. But his silence did not protect him. When, at the beginning of 1926, he struck up an alliance with Zinoviev and Kamenev who had broken with Stalin the year before, he became a target for the men in power.

In a press where only one voice could be heard, Trotsky was presented as the enemy within. He was accused of spreading a defeatist spirit in the Party, of divisive demagogy, and of planning the creation of a 'second party', neither proletarian nor Leninist, and of exhibiting 'social-democratic deviation'. In the middle of this top-level debate – during which he appeared before the leaders of the bureaucratic hierarchy – he was accused of 'maligning' the Party by speaking of a 'Thermidorian danger', and of a 'semi-defeatism in the face of the Imperialist threat': Stalin, at a crisis moment in British-Soviet relations, spoke of a 'single front from Chamberlain to Trotsky', and *Pravda* of the 'field-marshal' who led an 'anti-Bolshevik bloc' and spread 'revolting lies'.

In 1927, Trotsky was expelled for having 'led a factional campaign against the Party and its unity, tending towards the creation of a new anti-Leninist party in league with bourgeois intellectuals'. He was expelled from the USSR for having 'led counter-revolutionary demonstrations' and drawn attention to the 'Bonapartist danger' in a text distributed clandestinely.

The 1930s were the years in which the lies and accusations multiplied. Trotsky's books disappeared from libraries, his face from photographs, paintings and films, his name from history books and memoirs. The historians were whipped into line; they knew that not only their career, but their freedom and even their lives depended on their servility and on 'forgetting' Trotsky. At the same time, he was alluded to by the leaders as the incarnation of Evil.

At the first Moscow Trial, prosecutor Vyshinsky, Stalin's mouthpiece, accused him of having 'rolled in the filth of the White Guard', of mixing with the 'worst enemies of Soviet power', of being the 'organizing catalyst for the last remnants of the exploitative classes now annihilated in the USSR'. After it, millions of propagandists in all countries accused Trotsky of 'counting on the war and the defeat of Soviet power', and of preparing the assassination of its leaders, having already more or less effected that of Kirov.

In 1937, Vyshinsky accused him in the second Moscow Trial of plotting to 'take power with the aid of foreign States with the aim of re-establishing capitalist relations in the USSR', and of intensifying, with this aim in view, 'acts of diversion, sabotage and terrorism' in league with the Nazis. He confirmed the existence of a secret pact between Trotsky and Rudolf Hess, Hitler's lieutenant, that provided for the secession of territories. He accused Trotsky of having plotted sabotage and assassination attempts, acts of espionage and of laying false trails.

Such was the image in Russia of Trotsky, who lived out the last three years of his life in Mexico. The third Trial sought to fill in the lacunae left during the preceding ones, by producing culprits and witnesses that 'proved' Trotsky's links with the Gestapo and his old friend Rakovsky's dealings with the Intelligence Service.

Trotsky's murder in August 1940 by a Stalinist agent explains the escalation of accusations and calumnies. But it did not stop *Pravda* from assuring its readers that the murder had been carried out by 'one of his own disciples'...

In the remaining years of Stalin's reign, the figure of Trotsky became at once that of a 'non-person' and that of the 'Great Satan'. Ousted from his role, struck out of history and literature, stripped of his works and speeches – which were systematically omitted or attributed to others – erased from every kind of document, he sometimes emerges at the sting of a venomous note at the foot of some page conforming to the Stalinist gospel, appearing as the famous *Abbreviated*.

With the death of Stalin, everything changed again, as the skein of history started to rewind on its spool, and Trotsky's face re-emerged from the obscurity of the years of calumny.

The denunciation of Stalin's 'abuses' and 'personality cult', decided on by his successors and brought to its conclusion by Khrushchev did not automatically ensure the reappearance, and still less the rehabilitation of Trotsky. However, his position as the *Abbreviated* was no longer tenable. Necessitated by the desire to separate Lenin from Stalin, the publication of Lenin's Testament and Letters – a matter long contested – re-opened the 'Trotsky question'. Once Molotov had been accused of 'fabricating' an attempt on his own life, how could they not rehabilitate the man who had paid for this attack with his life, the Trotskyist Muralov?

After Khrushchev, Trotsky still remained the Big Bad Villain, but less diabolically so. Whereas the *Abbreviated* had consciously championed the restoration of capitalism, the 1961 *History of the Communist Party in the Soviet Union* claimed that he wanted to implement a line which 'would, finally, have led to the restoration of capitalism', which was a subtle retraction. Pressurized in organized debates by the old Bolshevik survivors, now rehabilitated, the historians ended up by painting a more complex portrait in the third volume of the Official History.

The historian Nancy Whittier Heer, who has painstakingly reconstructed the dossier, concluded that Trotsky was no longer regarded as 'a spy or a traitor', but as 'a personal disaster for the cause he served'. As he was no longer a 'non-person', Soviet readers were nevertheless able to follow his career. He became 'a partial or semi-person', as Mrs Heer puts it; maintaining such an image in suspension was a difficult task: it has lasted nearly a quarter of a century.

Trotsky's image, and the skein of history along with it, has been moving again since 1987. The important thing is not that Gorbachev mentioned him in his 70th Anniversary speech, treating him as the Stalinists treated him in 1926. Nor even, perhaps, that his portrait has been reinstalled in the Lenin Museum. The crucial thing is that a historian such as Yuri Afanassiev has recognized publicly that two conflicting versions of the history of the October Revolution exist in the USSR: the official version of the manuals and, we might add, of the bureaucrats, and that of the people, transmitted by word of mouth down from grandfather and grandmother.

The important matter revolves around Trotsky. It entails Dr Volobuiev's recognition of his historic role. It entails the denunciation of Vyshinsky by Vaksberg in the *Literatourniaia Gazeta*, and of the indictment of Stalin put in Trotsky's mouth in *Dalche, dalche...* by the playwright Chatrov. It entails, finally, the rehabilitation of his friend Rakovsky.

These signs show that the time is approaching when Trotsky will recover his true stature in the USSR, and everyone will have access to his writings without constraint or fear.

The Trotsky question will in the end be decided by the Soviet people itself. We hope that this book will be one of the items – modest but necessary – on which it rests its final judgement.

Chronology

This chronology is deliberately simplified over the first decades, and becomes detailed only in the context of the Mexican years.

1879
8 November: birth of Leon Davidovich Bronstein.

1897
Founding of the South Russian Workers' Union, organized by LD and his friends the Sokoloskys.

1898
28 January: LD and his friends arrested.
February: transferred to the prison at Kherson.
March: transferred to a prison in Odessa.

1900
Married in Moscow prison to Alexandra Lvovna Sokolovskaya.
Transferred to Siberia: Ust-Kut, then Verkholensk.

1902
With his wife's encouragement, LD escapes to Irkutsk, leaving her and his two small daughters behind.
October: meets Lenin in London. Has taken alias of 'Trotsky'.

1903
Meets Natalia Sedova in Paris. She becomes his second wife, and they later have two sons, Lyova and Sergei.
30 July-23 August: second Russian Social Democratic Party congress in Brussels, then London. Trotsky, originally faithful to Lenin, joins the 'Mensheviks' against the 'Bolsheviks' led by Lenin.

1905
Returns to Russia. Trotsky becomes the inspiration, scribe and orator of the Soviet of St Petersburg.

1912

18-30 January: Prague Conference. The Bolsheviks (Lenin) and the Mensheviks (Plekhanov) both claim to be the Party.

February: Trotsky denounces Lenin's factionalism.

1917

August: sixth national congress of the Bolsheviks. Trotsky becomes member of the Bolshevik Central Committee.

The Party increases its membership tenfold, passing the 200,000 mark.

23 September: Trotsky elected President of the Petrograd Soviet; he invites Kerensky's Provisional Government to quit.

7 November: in the name of the Military Revolutionary Committee, Trotsky declares that the Provisional Government has ceased to exist. Departure of the Mensheviks and the Socialist Revolutionaries from the Congress of Soviets. Storming of the Winter Palace by the Bolsheviks.

1918

January: peace negotiations with the Germans at Brest Litovsk. Lenin favours accepting the German conditions, Bukharin favours a 'revolutionary war', and Trotsky's motto is 'neither peace nor war'.

10 February: Trotsky announces 'We are withdrawing from the war'.

13 March: Trotsky becomes Commissar of War, and President of the Supreme War Council.

1919

2-7 March: foundation congress of the Communist International (Third International/Comintern). Trotsky writes the Manifesto.

25 July: Trotsky, his entourage and Stalin are awarded the Order of the Red Banner.

1920

August: The Red Army turned back at Warsaw.

1921

January-February: Debates over autonomy of trade unions. Zinoviev and Stalin side with Lenin against Trotsky, and advocate a policy that allows the working class to defend itself against the State and what Lenin calls its 'bureaucratic distortions'.

28 February: Kronstadt rising.

17-18 March: Kronstadt attacked and taken; the assailants sustain severe losses; massive reprisals in the fortress when it is finally taken.

1922

27 March-2 April: Trotsky supports Lenin against criticism from the Workers' Opposition at the Eleventh Congress. Stalin becomes General Secretary of the Communist Party.

November: Lenin proposes to Trotsky that they form a 'bloc against bureaucracy in general and the organizational branch in particular'.

25 December: Lenin's Testament refers to Trotsky and Stalin as the two most eminent leaders of the Central Committee, and suggests how schismatic conflict between them might be avoided.

1923

4 January: Lenin adds a postscript to his Testament recommending that Stalin be removed from his post as General Secretary.

8 October: Trotsky's letter denouncing the 'party regime' in the Politburo, and the 'bureaucratization' of its machinery.

1924

21 January: death of Lenin.

26 January: Lenin's state funeral and Stalin's oration; Trotsky, misinformed as to its date, does not return from Georgia.

October: publication of 'The Lessons of October', Trotsky's preface to his collected writings of 1917. Start of the smear campaign against him. His defence, 'Our Differences', is not published. Stalin characterizes 'old' and 'new' Trotskyism as inimical to Leninism, and develops his notion of 'Socialism in One Country'.

1927

March: Trotsky criticizes the Chinese policy of the leadership and the surrender of the Chinese CP to the Nationalist Kuomintang.

15 November: Trotsky and Zinoviev expelled from the Party for 'counter-revolutionary activities'.

1928

12 January: the GPU informs Trotsky of his banishment to Alma-Ata.

16 January: Zinoviev and Kamenev condemn Trotsky's 'schismatic' tendencies.

9 June: Nina, Trotsky's younger daughter, dies of consumption.

16 December: the GPU threatens Trotsky with reprisals if he continues with his political activities.

1929

20 January: the GPU informs Trotsky that he is expelled from the USSR under article 58/10 for 'preparing an armed struggle against Soviet power'.

12 February: having crossed on the *Ilyitch*, Trotsky with Natalia and Lyova disembark at Constantinople. For several months Trotsky seeks in vain for a European visa.

April: the Trotskys settle on the island of Prinkipo, in the Sea of Marmara.

16-23 April: the Central Committee condemns the 'Right deviation'.

23-29 April: the 16th Party Congress decides to backdate the beginning of the First Five Year Plan to 1 October 1928.

3 July: Molotov replaces Bukharin as head of the Comintern.

13 July: surrender of Radek, Preobrazhensky, Smilga. Panic among the ranks of deportees. First number of the *Bulletin of the Opposition* published in Berlin.

13 September: first number of *La Vérité*.

25 September: Trotsky approves Rakovsky's declaration of 22 August.

4 October: Rakovsky opposes 'radical collectivization'.

3 November: surrender of I.N. Smirnov and M. Boguslavsky, followed by hundreds of deportations.

10-17 November: Bukharin, Rykov and Tomsky make their self-criticism before the Central Committee, and are expelled from the Politburo.

27 December: Stalin declares himself in favour of the 'liquidation of the Kulaks as a class'.

1930

28 February: birth of the Belgian Left Opposition.

2 March: Stalin condemns the excesses of collectivization in his *Pravda* article, 'Dizzy with Success'.

30 March: birth of the United German Left Opposition (VLO).

6 April: International Bureau formed at Opposition conference in Paris.

12 April: Rakovsky's second declaration.

5 May: three leaders of the Italian CP – Tresso, Leonetti, Ravazzoli – turn to Trotsky.

June: beginning of the crisis in the French Section of the Opposition.

30 June: birth of the Argentine Opposition.

26 June-13 July: Sixteenth Party Congress. Tomsky expelled from the Politburo.

15 November: Chen Tu-Hsiu (the 'grand old man' of Chinese Marxism) writes open letter in Trotsky's favour.

3 December: Austrian Left Opposition breaks with the International Opposition.

December: unmasking of a 'leftist' group in the Russian CP, naming Shatskin, Sten and Lominadze (leaders of the 'young Stalinists'), together with Syrtsov and Chaplin.

1931

8 January: Zinaida and her five-year-old son Seva arrive on Prinkipo.

18 February: Lyova leaves Prinkipo for Berlin.

1 March: fire in the villa, destroying most of the family's belongings.

1 April: Trotskys move to Kodikoy, outside Constantinople.

May: meetings in Berlin between I.N. Smirnov and Lyova.

31 May: schism in the German Section.

8 August: Prussian plebiscite concerning the Social Democratic Government – Nazis and Communists unite in the 'Red Referendum'.

October: Greek Archiomarxist Organization joins the International Opposition.

26 October: Zinaida arrives in Berlin.

1932

January: Trotskys return to Prinkipo (Büyük Ada).

20 February: Stalin issues decree stripping Trotsky of Soviet nationality.

April: schism in the French Communist League, and birth of the Communist Left.

June: opposition blocs formed in the USSR.

August: circulation of the Riutin-Slepkov anti-Stalinist platform.

September: I. Smirnov, via E.S. Golzman, sends memorandum to Lyova concerning collectivization and state of USSR. Indication that Smirnov and friends wanted a 'bloc' with Trotsky, at least for information exchange.

135

19 October: Trotsky writes on the second expulsion of Zinoviev and Kamenev from the Party, authorised because they had read the Riutin-Slepkov platform and not condemned it.

14 November: Trotsky leaves for Copenhagen.

23 October: lectures to Danish Social Democratic students on the fifteenth anniversary of the October revolution.

12 December: Trotsky returns to Prinkipo.

1933

January: numerous arrests of former 'capitulators' in USSR, among them I.N. Smirnov.

4 January: Trotsky asks Germans to expel Roman Well, a Stalinist agent.

5 January: Zinaida commits suicide in Berlin.

6 January: the Chilean CP rallies the Left Opposition.

30 January: Hitler becomes Chancellor of Germany.

4-8 February: international conference of the Left Opposition, preceding Comintern and CPs' reaffirmation of the 'reform' and 'recovery' line.

12 February: Trotsky advocates a 'new Communist Party' in Germany.

27 February: Reichstag fire. Start of the systematic destruction of workers' organizations in Germany.

8 March: Victor Serge arrested and deported.

5 April: the Praesidium of the Comintern approves the policy line of the German CP which helped Hitler to power.

14 July: Nazis become sole political party in Germany.

15 July: Trotsky declares that a Fourth International should be founded.

17-24 July: Trotsky leaves for France and arrives in Marseilles.

26 July: settles in Saint-Palais, on the Atlantic coast.

August: meetings with representatives of leftist socialist organizations, e.g. Jacob Walcher of the Sozialistische Arbeiterpartei, Maring-Sneevliet of the Dutch Independent Socialist Party, André Malraux.

16-27 August: Paris conference of the Independent Socialist parties. German Sozialistische Arbetierpartei, two Dutch groups and the Trotskyists ('the Four') declare in favour of the Fourth International.

14 September: birth of the Bolshevik-Leninist Party in Cuba.

10-31 October: Trotsky and Natalia on holiday at Bagnères-de-Bigorre, Pyrenees.

1 November: settle in Barbizon.

30 December: conference of the Four in Paris.

1934

January-February: Trotsky participates secretly in French political life; congress of the 'victors' in Moscow i.e. those who had defeated opposition and achieved collectivization.

6 February: semi-insurrection of right-wing leagues in Paris in wake of the Stavisky Affair.

9 February: capitulation of Sosnovsky.

12 February: French general strike with united workers' front. Beginning of Nazi press campaign accusing Trotsky of being behind the agitation in France.

23 February: Rakovsky finally capitulates.

14 April: the Melun *Procureur* 'discovers' Trotsky's presence in Barbizon.

16 April: judicial order expelling Trotsky cannot take effect as he has no visa. He wanders from place to place in France for over two months.

June: from Saint-Pierre-de-Chartreuse, Trotsky encourages his comrades to join the SFIO (French Socialist Party): this move known as *entrisme* or the 'French turn'.

10 July: settles in Domesne, near Grenobles.

September: Opposition crisis over the *entrisme* question.

1-2 December: the fusion of the AWP and the CLA gives rise to the Workers' Party of the United States (WPUS).

1 December: S. Kirov, head of the Leningrad organization and Politburo member, assassinated. Imposition of emergency measures.

4 December: sixty-six executions on pretext of Kirov's murder.

16 December: Zinoviev, Kamenev and others arrested for the murder of Kirov.

25 December: birth of the Swiss Section, MAS.

28 December: Nikolaev and his fellow 'conspirators' sentenced to death.

29 December: execution of nineteen 'Kirov assassins'.

1935

15-18 January: trial of Zinoviev (sentenced to ten years) and Kamenev (five years) for 'moral responsibility' for Kirov's assassination.

23 January: sentencing of leaders of the Leningrad GPU.

1 February: N.I. Yezhov becomes secretary of the CC and member

of the Party Control Commission; waves of arrests.

2-3 March: the two Dutch parties, the RSP and the OSP, join to form the RSAP.

10 March: the Belgian Section elects to join the Belgian Workers' Party.

8 April: the death sentence in the USSR made applicable to children under sixteen.

15 May: Pierre Laval signs Franco-Soviet non-aggression pact, and returns with declaration of Stalin's support for French defence policy.

25 May: Society of Old Bolsheviks disbanded.

7 June: A. Enukidze, Secretary of the Central Soviet Executive, expelled from the Party.

9 June: families declared to share responsibility in penal matters in USSR.

10 June: Trotskys leave Domesne.

18 June: Trotskys in Oslo.

23 June: Trotskys settle in the home of K. Knudsen in Vexhall.

25 July-20 August: the Seventh Comintern Congress elects to generalize the policy of the Popular Front.

27 July: second sentencing of Kamenev held in secret.

31 July: expulsion of the leaders of the Young Socialists, Seine Section.

19 September-20 October: Trotsky in hospital.

18 November: schism in the Dutch RSAP.

6 December: publication of paper *La Commune* advocating disaffiliation from the SFIO results in Trotsky's break with R. Molinier.

20-22 December: Trotsky on ski-ing trip in wilds of Norway – had to be rescued when trapped by snow.

1936

16 February: electoral victory of Popular Front in Spain.

21-24 February: founding Congress of the Confederation of Mexican Workers.

1 March: the WPUS Congress elects to join the US Socialist Party.

7 March: remilitarization of the Rhineland. Founding of the Independent CP by Molinier and Frank.

30 March: end of the Chilean Frente Popular.

1 April: fusion of the YS and YC in Spain to form the YSU.

26 April: first electoral round in France favours the SFIO and the CP.

3 May: electoral victory of the Popular Front in France.

26 May: beginning of the French 'strikes of '36'.

31 May: joint congress of the Bolshevik-Leninist Group and the Young Revolutionary Socialist Party; birth of the French POR (Workers Revolutionary Party).

4 June: Léon Blum forms government.

7 June: signing of the Matignon agreements.

21 June: first 'confessions' of I. Smirnov, still denying the terrorist acts of which he has been accused.

6 July: new constitution in the USSR.

14 July: petrol workers on strike in Mexico.

18-20 July: Spanish military uprising under generals including Franco. Start of Civil War.

29-31 July: 'Geneva Conference' in Paris and creation of movement for the Fourth International.

5-6 August: followers of Quisling raid Knudsen's house while he and Trotsky on holiday.

19-24 August: First Moscow Trial: sixteen executed, among them Zinoviev, Kamenev and Smirnov who had publicly 'confessed'.

29 August: Trotsky's two secretaries deported.

2 September: Trotsky and Natalia interned in Norway.

4 September: Popular Front government under the Socialist Largo Caballero set up in 'Republican' Spain.

22 September: Radek arrested.

26 September: Andres Nin, leader of the POUM, becomes Councillor of Justice in Catalonia. Yagoda replaced by Yezhov as head of GPU.

3 October: founding of Belgian Revolutionary Socialist Party.

22 October: American Committee for the Defence of Leon Trotsky set up in New York.

27 October: Trotskyist deportees in Vorkuta begin a hunger strike that lasts four months.

7 November: break-in at the Paris office where Trotsky kept his papers.

15 November: petrol workers strike.

7 December: the Mexican president, Lazaro Cárdenas, announces that he has granted Trotsky a Mexican visa.

19 December: Trotsky and Natalia embark on the tanker *Ruth*.

1937

9 January: arrival at Tampico.

11 January: arrival at Coyoacán, where they settle in Frida Kahlo's Blue House.

21 January: Lyova Sedov misses a rendezvous at Mulhouse, where GPU killers were lying in wait for him.

23-30 January: Second Moscow Trial: Radek, Piatakov and Muralov executed.

19 February: Jan Fraenkel, Trotsky's former secretary, arrives in Mexico.

1 March: formation of Joint Commission of Inquiry into the Moscow Trials, to be chaired by John Dewey.

10-17 April: preliminary commission inquiry at Coyoacán, and Trotsky's statement.

21 April: Comintern secret conference on the fight against Trotskyism.

3-6 May: workers' rising in Barcelona.

15 May: Largo Caballero resigns.

17 May: Negrín government in Spain, considered to be in thrall to Stalin.

12 June: after discovery of Tukhachevsky 'conspiracy', the Commander-in-Chief of the Red Army executed; prelude to purge of army affecting 25,000 officers.

16 June: arrest of POUM leaders in Spain.

24 June: Cárdenas nationalizes Mexican railways.

26-30 June: Earl Browder, head of American CP, insists to the Mexican CP that there should be 'unity at all costs', together with Lombardo Toledano (head of CMW, Confederation of Mexican Workers); both groups strongly opposed to Trotsky.

3-4 July: Dutch RSAP breaks with the Fourth International.

July: Ignaz Reiss, chief of a Soviet secret service network, resigns his post, gets message to Lyova describing process of purges; sends letter to Central Committee announcing his break with Stalinism and new loyalty to Fourth International.

7-26 July: Trotsky stays at San Miguel Regla.

31 July: Erwin Wolf, Trotsky's secretary in Norway, arrested in Barcelona on the eve of his departure.

19 August: release of Chen Tu-hsiu in China.

4 September: Reiss's body found near Lausanne.

13 September: Wolf killed by GPU.

28 September: Joe Hansen arrives in Coyoacán.

20 October: Fraenkel leaves.

7 November: unification of Argentinian Trotskyists.

13 December: Dewey Commission announces its verdict, acquitting Trotsky and Sedov of Moscow's accusations.

31 December: beginning of Socialist Workers' Party Congress, founded by the American partisans of Trotsky expelled from the SP.

1938

13 February: unification of Czech groups.

16 February: L. Sedov dies in Paris.

29 February: CMW Congress votes a resolution against Trotsky and Trotskyism.

2-13 March: Third Moscow Trial. Execution of Bukharin, Rykov, Yagoda; Rakovsky imprisoned.

11 March: Germany annexes Austria – the *Anschluss.*

18 March: Cárdenas government expropriates the oil companies in Mexico.

23 March: enormous demonstration supporting Cárdenas against the threats of powers who deemed nationalizations contrary to their interests.

30 March: birth of the official Mexican Revolutionary Party, of which the CMW is a part.

Spring: Trotskyists in the Vorkuta labour camp executed group by group.

16 May: revolt of General Cedillo against Cárdenas.

10 July: Trotsky, Rivera and Breton at Patzcuaro.

14 July: Rudolf Klement, Trotsky's secretary at Barbizon and secretary of proposed International, killed by GPU.

3 September: conference at Rosmer's home in Périgny; proclamation of the Fourth International.

22 September: general strike in Prague against the government, which gives in to Germany.

29 September: Munich Conference and Agreement.

7 October: Trotsky predicts a Hitler-Stalin pact.

11-31 October: trial of surviving POUM leaders (Andres Nin had been kidnapped and murdered).

20 December: internal passports made mandatory in the USSR.

1939

7 January: Rivera quits the Fourth International.

25 January: Franco's troops enter Barcelona.

26 January: anti-Semitic demonstrations against Trotsky in Mexico.

February: series of executions of old Bolsheviks in Moscow.

March: after quarrel with Rivera, Trotskys leave the Blue House for house in Calle Viena.

10-21 March: Eighteenth Congress of the CPSU.

22 March: Marguerite Rosmer locates Seva Volkov in a religious house.

28 March: Franco's troops enter Madrid.

8 August: Seva arrives in Coyoacán with the Rosmers.

22 August: Nazi-Soviet pact.

1 September: German army enters Poland; war is declared.

3 September: Burnham demands the start of an open discussion on 'the nature of the USSR'.

17 September: Red Army enters Poland.

28 September: second Nazi-Soviet pact.

12 October: Ramón Mercader enters Mexico. The Dies Committee (investigating 'un-American activities') invites Trotsky to testify.

26-28 October: West Ukrainian (ex-Polish) National Assembly applies to join USSR.

28-30 October: West Belorussian (ex-Polish) National Assembly applies to join USSR.

30 November: Red Army attacks Finland.

12 December: Senator Dies withdraws his invitation to Trotsky.

13 December: SWP minority publishes *War and Bureaucratic Conservatism*.

1940

25 January: commission to purge the Mexican CP.

27 January: Trotsky writes his will. Laborde and Campa expelled from MCP.

1 February: Burnham writes *Science and Style* against Trotsky.

12 March: armistice between Finland and the USSR.

5-9 April: at the SWP Congress, the 'majority' (Trotskyists, led by James P. Cannon) defeat the 'minority' (Burnham and Schachtman).

17 April: the SWP minority make off with the Party journal, *The New International* and the group splits.

1 May: demonstration organized by CWM in Mexico City: 'Out with Trotsky' on the banners.

10 May: German offensive in the West.

19 May: beginning of emergency conference, New York.

21 May: Burnham resigns from the SWP.

24 May: failed attack on Trotsky's house.

26 May: second emergency conference in New York and adoption of manifesto.

28 May: Ramón Mercader's first visit to the Trotskys.

22 June: Franco-German armistice.

25 June: discovery of corpse of Robert Sheldon Harte, Trotsky's bodyguard, missing since 24 May.

3-6 August: Baltic States 'voluntarily' join USSR.

20 August: Mercader attacks Trotsky in his office.

21 August: death of Leon Trotsky.